THE GIFT
OF SUFFERING

THE

GIFT

OF SUFFERING

F.B. MEYER

Selected and edited by WILLIAM J. PETERSEN

Introduction by *MERRILL WOMACH*

Illustrations by *RON McCARTY*

KEATS PUBLISHING, INC.   NEW CANAAN, CONNECTICUT

THE GIFT OF SUFFERING

Shepherd Illustrated Classic edition published in 1980

Selection and special contents of this edition
copyright © 1980 by Keats Publishing, Inc.

Library of Congress Catalog Card Number: 79-93432
ISBN: 0-87983-211-8

Printed in the United States of America

SHEPHERD ILLUSTRATED CLASSICS are published by Keats
Publishing, Inc. 36 Grove Street, New Canaan, Connecticut 06840

CONTENTS

Illustrations

Introduction to the Shepherd
Classics Edition

In the many miles we travel in our concert tours across the country, and the thousands of Christians we talk with, the most frequently asked question is, "Why do Christians have to suffer?" For all of us find ourselves asking this question as we view our troubled families, friends, neighbors, or ourselves. I would like to suggest this book, *The Gift of Suffering*, as I believe it is one of the greatest books ever written on the subject of "why Christians suffer."

The truth found in this book will not only be helpful to one who has passed through suffering, but also to those who are presently being tested, or who will soon face a severe trial.

It is my belief that this book is one that should be read by all Christians as it not only deals with the reasons for suffering, but also points out the very positive aspects of the times of severe trials in the life of a Christian. One cannot read these pages without being drawn nearer to our great God and Savior, Jesus Christ, and understand in a new way His great love for us.

With Divine Inspiration, the author unfolds to us through the use of the Holy Scripture, not only God's love, but His eternal purpose in our lives. Meyer points out that life can have meaning, that you can experience perfect peace, you can awake and sing, as you put your trust completely in the Lord.

The author's motto for Happy Living is one of the best I have ever read and comes directly from the Word of God. He recognizes that the complete life is found in submission of our will to God's will; having the mind of Christ in us, being constantly aware of His eternal presence and His unfailing love and being led continually by the example of Christ.

"Looking unto Jesus the author and finisher of our faith; who for the joy that was set before him endured the cross, despising the shame, and is set down at the right had of the throne of God" (Hebrews 12:2).

MERRILL WOMACH
January, 1980

THE
GIFT
OF
SUFFERING

The writings of

F.B. Meyer

THE GIFT OF SUFFERING

"For unto you it is given in the behalf of Christ, not only to believe on him, but also to suffer for his sake."

PHILIPPIANS 1:29

THE LOVE OF GOD in Jesus Christ could only display itself through suffering, and the love of God to-day can only display itself and work out its higher purposes through suffering. Therefore it is given to us, on the behalf of the enthroned Lamb, not only to believe on Him, but to suffer for His name.

The word translated "It is given" betokens a kingly gift. It is as though the Son of God, in the execution of the Divine purpose that fills His heart, were passing through the world to-day selecting certain souls that are akin to His own, and with a royal smile upon His face bending over them communicating this supreme benefaction. And happy is it for any men or women who have this supreme honor of believing and suffering.

As for believing, we believe that in Jesus Christ God has come into this selfish world to set up the standard of universal love. We believe that the cross, whatever else it was in the way of substitution and satisfaction for sin, was the triumph of redemption. We look upon it that this world is already a redeemed world, and that Jesus Christ has won the right to rule in every department of our life. This is our faith to-day, and this is what the world is waiting for.

Side by side with that general creed there is our personal faith in Him. For what is faith? Faith is the union of the soul with God; faith is the subordination of the whole nature to the unseen Spirit of Christ, that He may achieve through the yielded manhood His perfect

3

conceptions. Faith unites herself first with the purpose of God, ascertaining what that purpose is, and then faith yields herself in absolute abandonment that God may realize that purpose. Faith counts not her worth, for she is conscious that she is absolutely helpless apart from Him. Faith looks not into the future to calculate the results. Faith fears not the frown, nor does she seek the praise of men. Her one thought is the exalted and the unseen Christ, Who Himself has suffered, and by suffering has laid the foundations of the temple of perfect love; and following Him she is prepared, even unto blood and tears, to yield everything to Him that He may achieve His purpose.

But we are not only called to believe in Him with the creed and the personal loyalty, but to suffer. In the first days, those great days of the early Church, when she broke upon the world as a dream of beauty, with her conceptions of immortality and of God, men understood that this was part of the program, and they were proud when they had the honor of sealing their testimony with their blood. In the early Church, edicts had to be promulgated to restrain the early Christians from martyrdom. I have sometimes seen pictures of burials in the Catacombs, as though the early Christians stealthily and with downcast heads carried the mangled corpses of the martyrs for sepulture. I have no faith that that was their bearing. I believe they went as conquerors; I believe they went with songs of victory upon their lips, as they carried to their last resting-place the bodies of those who had been counted worthy to suffer for His name.

And there is suffering still. We should not be in the track of those who have preceded us unless we were prepared to suffer; the Church would have lost one of the marks of her apostolicity unless she shed tears of blood to-day. It is the martyr Church which is going to win the empire of God.

The suffering will come to us thus. There is a suffering that every man has in his own inner life as he does violence to himself, and as day by day he mercilessly bruises his antagonist. Every man wears the hair shirt next his skin; there is the constant daily agony of the cross. There is also the suffering that we have as with Jesus we learn obedience by the things that we suffer, and are perfected as we accept God's discipline in life. And there is the suffering we have, the passion for the souls of men.

We read of Brainerd sweating in the cold wind in the forest on a winter's day, as he pleaded for the souls of his Indians. We think of men who have wrestled on the hillsides of Scotland in the old Convenanting days, and of those who in every land have poured out their souls in a very agony for others. Just as in natural birth none is born except at the cost of travail, I believe that no soul is ever born into the Kingdom of God except we know something of the sufferings of Christ as we travail for it. But in addition to those three there is suffering which must come in our collision with the selfishness of the world. Why did Jesus suffer on the human side? Was it not because He brought the love of God, and He proposed to apply that to all the conditions of mankind; and the priests and the rulers said, "We will have none of it; He will undermine our power; He will take away our authority and gain"—and Jesus was crucified on the human side because He insisted that the love of God was the one rule for men. And if you and I are going to apply that principle, there is not one of us that will not have to suffer. The minister will have to suffer as he seeks to apply that principle to the family, the social and

5

the business life of his people. The Churches are quite prepared to admit that Christianity is a good thing as a theory, but too often, when you begin to apply it to the details of human life, men squirm. Then comes the inevitable suffering; then the Church is again crucified with her Lord, and fills up that which is behind of His sufferings.

I have a vision of our King. He was the Lamb slain before the foundation of the world. He bears to-day upon His flesh the marks of Calvary; He is the One who, for the love of God and to make God's love supreme, yielded His life. He looks down from His throne upon us, nay, He is in our midst, and we here pledge ourselves to Him again to follow Him, to realize His purpose among men. Let the suffering come, let the cup be put to our lips. So shall it be to the end. It is *given* to us.

HOW TO BEAR SORROW

"Who comforteth us in all our tribulation, that we may be able to comfort them which are in any trouble, by the comfort wherewith we ourselves are comforted of God."

II CORINTHIANS 1:4

YOU are passing through a time of deep sorrow. The love on which you were trusting has suddenly failed you, and dried up like a brook in the desert—now a dwindling stream, then shallow pools, and at last drought You are always listening for footsteps that do not come, waiting for a word that is not spoken, pining for a reply that tarries overdue.

Perhaps the savings of your life have suddenly disappeared; instead of helping others, you must be helped, or you must leave the warm nest where you have been sheltered from life's storms to go alone into an unfriendly world; or you are suddenly called to assume the burden of some other life, taking no rest for yourself till you have steered it through dark and difficult seas into the haven. Your health, or sight, or nervous energy is failing; you carry in yourself the sentence of death; and the anguish of anticipating the future is almost unbearable. In other cases there is the sense of recent loss through death, like the gap in the forest-glade, where the woodsman has lately been felling trees.

At such times life seems almost insupportable. Will every day be as long as this? Will the slow moving hours ever again quicken their pace? Will life ever array itself in another garb than the torn autumn remnants of past summer glory? Hath God forgotten to be gracious? Hath

9

He in anger shut up His tender mercies? Is His mercy clean gone for ever?

This road has been trodden by myriads.—When you think of the desolating wars which have swept through every century and devastated every land; of the expeditions of the Nimrods, the Nebuchadnezzars, the Timours, the Napoleons of history; of the merciless slave-trade, which has never ceased to decimate Africa; and of all the tyranny, the oppression, the wrong which the weak and defenseless have suffered at the hands of their fellows; of the unutterable sorrows of women and children, surely you must see that by far the larger number of our race have passed through the same bitter griefs as those which rend your heart. Jesus Christ Himself trod this difficult path, leaving traces of His blood on its flints; and apostles, prophets, confessors, and martyrs have passed by the same way. It is comforting to know that others have traversed the same dark valley, and that the great multitudes that stand before the Lamb, wearing palms of victory, came out of great tribulation. Where they were, we are; and by God's grace, where they are we shall be.

Do not talk about punishment.—You may talk of chastisement or correction, for our Father deals with us as with sons; or you may speak of reaping the results of mistakes and sins dropped as seeds into life's furrows in former years; or you may have to bear the consequences of the sins and mistakes of others; but do not speak of punishment. Surely all the guilt and penalty of sin were laid on Jesus, and He put them away for ever. His were the stripes, and the chastisement of our peace. If God punishes us for our sins, it would seem that the sufferings of Christ were incomplete; and if He once began to

10

punish us, life would be too short for the infliction of all that we deserve. Besides, how could we explain the anomalies of life, and the heavy sufferings of the saints as compared with the gay life of the ungodly? Surely, if our sufferings were penal, there would be a reversal of these lots.

Sorrow is a refiner's crucible.—It may be caused by the neglect or cruelty of another, by circumstances over which the sufferer has no control, or as the direct result of some dark hour in the long past; but inasmuch as God has permitted it to come, it must be accepted as His appointment, and considered as the furnace by which He is searching, testing, probing, and purifying the soul. Suffering searches us as fire does metals. We think we are fully for God, until we are exposed to the cleansing fire of pain; then we discover, as Job did, how much dross there is in us, and how little real patience, resignation, and faith. Nothing so detaches us from the things of this world, the life of sense, the bird-lime of earthly affections. There is probably no other way by which the power of the self-life can be arrested, that the life of Jesus may be manifested in our mortal flesh.

But God always keeps the discipline of sorrow in His own hands.—Our Lord said, "My Father is the husbandman." His hands hold the pruning-knife; His eye watches the crucible; His gentle touch is on the pulse while the operation is in progress. He will not allow even the devil to have his own way with us. As in the case of Job, so always. The moments are carefully allotted. The severity of the test is exactly determined by the reserves of grace and strength which are lying unrecognized within, but will be sought for and used beneath the severe pressure of pain. He holds the winds in His fist, and the waters in the hollow of His hand. He dare not risk the loss of that which has cost Him the blood of His Son. "God is faithful, who will not suffer you to be *tried* above that ye are able."

In sorrow the Comforter is near.—"Very present in time of trouble." He *sits* by the crucible as a Refiner of silver, regulating the heat, marking every change, waiting patiently for the scum to float away, and His own face to be mirrored in clear, translucent metal. No earthly friend may tread the winepress with you, but the Saviour is there, His garments stained with the blood of the grapes of your sorrow. Dare to repeat it often, though you do not feel it, and though Satan insists that God has left you, *"Thou art with me."* Mention His name again and again, *"Jesus*, JESUS, Thou art with me." So you will become conscious that He is there.

When friends come to console you they talk of time's healing touch, as though the best balm for sorrow were to forget, or in their well-meant kindness they suggest travel, diversion, amusement, and show their inability to appreciate the black night that hangs over your soul; so you turn from them, sick at heart, and prepared to say, as Job of his, "Miserable comforters are ye all." But all the while Jesus is nearer than they are, understanding how they wear you, knowing each throb of pain, touched by fellow-feeling, silent in a love too full to speak, waiting to comfort from hour to hour as a mother soothes her weary, suffering babe.

Be sure to study the art of this Divine comfort, that you may be able to comfort them that are in any affliction with the comfort with which you yourself have been comforted of God (2 Cor. I.4). There can be no doubt that some trials are permitted to come to us, as to our Lord, for no other reason than that by means of them we should become able to give sympathy and succour to others. And we should watch with all care each symptom of the pain, and each prescription of the Great Physician, since, in all probability, at some future time, we shall be called to minister to those passing through similar experiences. Thus we learn by the things that we suffer, and, being made perfect, become authors of priceless and eternal help to souls in agony.

Do not shut yourself up with your sorrow.—A friend, in the first anguish of bereavement, wrote, saying that he must give up the Christian ministries in which he had delighted; and I replied immediately, urging him not to do so, because there is no solace for heartpain like ministry. The temptation of great suffering is towards isolation, withdrawal from the life of men, sitting alone, and keeping silence. Do not yield to it. Break through the icy chains of reserve, if they have already gathered. Arise, anoint your head, and wash your face; go forth to do your duty, with willing though chastened steps. Selfishness, of every kind, in its activities or its introspection, is a hurtful thing, and shuts out the help and love of God. Sorrow is apt to be selfish. The soul occupied with its own griefs, and refusing to be comforted, becomes presently a Dead Sea, full of brine and salt, over which birds do not fly, and beside which no green thing grows. And thus we miss the very lesson that God would teach us. His constant war is against the self-life, and every pain he inflicts is to lessen its hold on us. But we may thwart His purpose, and extract poison from His

13

gifts, as men get opium and alcohol from innocent plants.

A Hindu woman, the beautiful Eastern legend tells us, lost her only child. Wild with grief, she implored a prophet to give back her little one to her love. He looked at her for a long while tenderly, and said, "Go, my daughter, bring me a handful of rice from a house into which Death has never entered, and I will do as thou desirest." The woman at once began her search. She went from dwelling to dwelling, and had no difficulty in obtaining what the prophet specified; but when they had granted it, she inquired, "Are you all here around the hearth—father, mother, children—none missing?" But the people invariably shook their heads with sighs and looks of sadness; for far and wide as she wandered, there was always some vacant seat by the hearth. And gradually, as she passed on, the narrator says, the waves of her grief subsided before the spectacle of sorrow everywhere, and her heart, ceasing to be occupied with its own selfish pang, flowed out in strong yearnings of sympathy with the universal suffering; tears of anguish softened into tears of pity, passion melted away in compassion, she forgot herself in the general interest, and found redemption in redeeming.

Do not chide yourself for feeling strongly.—Tears are natural. Jesus wept. A thunderstorm without rain is fraught with peril; the pattering raindrops cool the air, and relieve the overcharged atmosphere. The swollen brooks indicate that the snows are melting on the hills and spring is near. "Daughters of Jerusalem," said our Lord, "weep for yourselves and your children." To bear sorrow with dry eyes and stolid heart may befit a Stoic, but not a Christian. We have no need to rebuke fond nature

"Jesus wept"

crying for its mate, its lost joy, the touch of the vanished hand, the sound of the voice that is still, provided only that the will is resigned. This is the one consideration for those who suffer—*Is the will right?* If it isn't God Himself cannot comfort. If it is, then the path will inevitably lead from the valley of the shadow of death to the banqueting table and the overflowing cup.

Many say: I cannot feel resigned. It is bad enough to have my grief to bear, but I have this added trouble, that I cannot *feel* resigned. My invariable reply is: you probably never can feel resignation, but you can *will* it. The Lord Jesus, in the Garden of Gethsemane, has shown us how to suffer. He chose His Father's will. Though Judas, prompted by Satan, was the instrument for mixing the cup and placing it to the Saviour's lips, He looked right beyond him to the Father, who permitted him to work his cruel way, and said: "The cup that My Father giveth Me to drink, shall I not drink it?" And He said repeatedly, "If this cup may not pass from Me, except I drink it, Thy will be done." He gave up His own way and will, saying, "I will Thy will, O My Father; Thy will, and not Mine, be done."

Let all sufferers who read these lines go apart and dare to say the same words: "Thy will, and not mine; Thy will be done in the earth of my life, as in the heaven of Thy purpose; I choose Thy will." Say this thoughtfully and deliberately, not because you can feel it, but because you will it; not because the way of the cross is pleasant, but because it must be right. Say it repeatedly, whenever the surge of pain sweeps through you, whenever the wound begins to bleed afresh: Not my will, but Thine be done. *Dare to say Yes to God.*

15

"Even so, Father, for so it seemeth good in Thy sight."

And so you will be led to feel that all is right and well; and a great calm will settle down on your heart, a peace that passeth understanding, a sense of rest, which is not inconsistent with suffering, but walks in the midst of it as the three young men in the fiery furnace, to whom the burning coals must have been like the dewy grass of a forest glade. "The doctor told us our little child was dying. I felt like a stone. But *in a moment* I seemed to give up my hold on her. She appeared no longer mine, but God's."

Be sure to learn God's lessons.—Each sorrow carries at its heart a germ of holy truth, which, if you get and sow in the soil of your heart, will bear harvests of fruit, as seed-corns from mummy-cases fruit in English soil. God has a meaning in each blow of His chisel, each incision of His knife. He knows the way that He takes. But His object is not always clear to us.

In suffering and sorrow God touches the minor chords, develops the passive virtues, and opens to view the treasures of darkness, the constellations of promise, the rainbow of hope, the silver light of the convenant. What is character without sympathy, submission, patience, trust, and hope that grips the unseen as an anchor? But these graces are only possible through sorrow. Sorrow is a garden, the trees of which are laden with the peaceable fruits of righteousness; do not leave it without bringing them with you. Sorrow is a mine, the walls of which glisten with precious stones; be sure and do not retrace your steps into daylight without some specimens. Sorrow is a school. You are sent to sit on its hard benches and learn from its black-lettered pages lessons which will make you wise for ever; do not trifle away your chance of graduating there. Miss Havergal used to talk of "turned lessons"!

Count on the afterward.—God will not always be causing grief. He traverses the dull brown acres with His plough, seaming the yielding earth, that He may be able to cast in the precious grain. Believe that in days of sorrow He is sowing light for the righteous, and gladness for the upright in heart. Look forward to the reaping. Anticipate the joy which is set before you, and shall flood your heart with minstrel notes when patience has had her perfect work.

You will live to recognize the wisdom of God's choice for you. You will one day see that the thing you wanted was only second best. You will be surprised to remember that you once nearly broke your heart and spilt the wine of your life, for what would never have satisfied you, if you had caught it, as the child the butterfly or soap-bubble. You will meet again your beloved. You will have again your love. You will become possessed of a depth of character, a breadth of sympathy, a fund of patience, an ability to understand and help others, which, as you lay them at Christ's feet for Him to use, will make you glad that you were afflicted. You will see God's plan and purpose; you will reap His harvest; you will behold His face, and be satisfied. Each wound will have its pearl; each carcass will contain a swarm of bees; each foe, like Midian to Gideon, will yield its goodly spoil.

The way of the cross, rightly borne, is the only way to the everlasting light. The path that threads the Garden

17

of Gethsemane, and climbs over the hill of Calvary, alone conducts to the visions of the Easter morning and the glories of the Ascension mount. If we will not drink of His cup, or be baptised with His baptism, or fill up that which is behind of His sufferings, we cannot expect to share in the joy of His espousals and the ecstasy of His triumph. But if these conditions are fulfilled, we shall not miss one note in the everlasting song, one element in the bliss that is possible to men.

Remember that somehow suffering rightly borne enriches and helps mankind.—The death of Hallam was the birthday of Tennyson's *In Memoriam*. The cloud of insanity that brooded over Cowper gave us, *God moves in a mysterious way*. Milton's blunders taught him to sing of *Holy Light, offspring of heaven firstborn*. Rist used to say, "The dear cross has pressed many songs out of me." And it is probable that none rightly suffer anywhere without contributing something to the alleviation of human grief, to the triumph of good over evil, of love over hate, and of light over darkness.

If you believed this, could you not bear to suffer? Is not the chief misery of all suffering its loneliness, and perhaps its apparent aimlessness? Then dare to believe that no man dieth to himself. Fall into the ground, bravely and cheerfully to die; if you refuse this, you will abide alone, but if you yield to it, you will bear fruit which will sweeten the lot and strengthen the life of others who will never know your name, or stop to thank you for your help.

Human life is becoming richer as the generations pass, because each contributes its special ingredient to the general sum of good. The leaves fall unnoticed on the forest floor, and rot, but it grows richer. All suffering rightly borne fills up that which is behindhand of the sufferings of Christ, and helps, though it has no substitutionary value, to hasten the redemptive processes that work out from His Cross.

BUT LIFE IS SO BORING

"For even hereunto were ye called."

I PETER 2:21

A YOUNG FRIEND, richly gifted, but who is tied by inexorable necessity to an office stool, has complained to me that his life afforded no outlet for the adequate exercise of his powers.

His groan is a very common one. So many grumble about the monotony of life's dead-level, which the great majority of us have to traverse. The upland paths, which give an ecstasy to tread, in the bracing air, and the expanding glory of the world, are for the few. For most of us it is the trivial round, the common task. Each morning the bell calls to the same routine of commonplace toil. Each hour brings the same program of trifles. There seems no chance for doing anything heroic, which will be worth having lived for, or will shed a light back on all past, and forward on all coming days.

But there are two or three considerations which, if wrought into the heart, will tend to remove much of this terrible depression.

1. *All Life is Part of a Divine Plan.*—As a mother desires the best possible for her babes, bending over the cradle which each occupies in turn, so does God desire to do His best for us all. He hates nothing that He has made; but has a fair ideal for each, which He desires to accomplish in us with perfect love. But there is no way of transferring it to our actual experience, except by the

23

touch of His Spirit within, and the education of our circumstances without.

He has chosen the circumstances of our life, because they are the shortest path, if only we use them as we should, to reach the goal on which He has set His heart. He might have chosen some other country—China, India, Italy, or Mexico. He might have chosen some other age—that of the Flood, the Exodus, or of the early martyrs. He might have chosen some other lot—a royal court, a senate, a pulpit, or an author's desk. But since He chose this land, this age, and your lot, whatever it may be, we must believe that these presented the likeliest and swiftest way for realizing His purpose.

If, my brother, you could have reached your truest manhood as an emperor or a reformer, as a millionaire or a martyr, you would have been born into one of those positions; but since you are only a servant, a bank clerk, or an ordinary business man you will find right beside you the materials and possibilities of a great life.

If, my sister, you could have attained to the loftiest development of your nature by being a mother, or a rich man's wife, or a queen, you would have found yourself placed there; but since your lot is that of milliner's assistant, factory hand, or toiling mother, you must believe that somewhere within your reach, if only you will search for them, you will discover the readiest conditions of a noble and useful life.

Who can wonder at the complaints of the aimlessness, the vanity, the weariness of life? People either have no plan, or they have got a wrong one. "What's the fashion?"

"What do others do?" "What's the correct thing?" How much better and wiser to believe that God has a perfect plan for each of us, and that He is unfolding it a bit at a time, by the events which He puts into our life each day!

Before Moses built the Tabernacle, he saw the whole pattern of it in prophetic vision. In some secluded spot on Sinai's heights it stood before him, woven out of sunbeams; and he descended to the mountain foot to repeat it in actual curtains, gold, and wood. God does not show us the whole plan of our life at a burst, but unfolds it to us bit by bit. Each day He gives us the opportunity of weaving a curtain, carving a peg, fashioning the metal. We know not what we do. But at the end of our life the disjointed pieces will suddenly come together, and we shall see the symmetry and beauty of the Divine thought. Then we shall be satisfied. In the meantime let us believe that God's love and wisdom are doing the very best for us. In the morning ask God to show you His plan for the day in the unfolding of its events, and to give you grace to do or bear all that He may have prepared. In the midst of the day's engagements, often look up and say, "Father, is this in the plan?" At night be still, and match your actual with God's ideal, confessing your sins and shortcomings, and asking that His will may be more perfectly done in you, even as in heaven.

2. *Every Life affords Opportunities for Building up Noble Character.*—We are sent into this world to build up character which will be blessed and useful in that great future for which we are being trained. There is a niche which only we can fill, a crown which only we can wear,

music which only we can waken, service which only we can render. God knows what these are, and He is giving us opportunities to prepare for them. Life is our school-house. Its rooms may be bare, but they are littered with opportunities of becoming fit for our great inheritance.

Knitting needles are cheap and common enough, but on them may be wrought the fairest designs in the richest wools. So the incidents of daily life may be common-place in the extreme, but on them, as the material foundation, we may build the unseen but everlasting fabric of a noble and beautiful character. It does not so much matter what we do, but the way in which we do it matters greatly. What we do may or may not live; but the way in which we perform our common tasks becomes an inde-structible part of our character, for better or worse, and for ever.

Suppose we meet the daily demands of life in a slovenly and careless spirit, caring only to escape blame, to earn our wage, or to preserve a decent average. Or suppose our one aim in life is to get money for our own enjoyment. Is it not clear that the meanness of the motive will react on the whole character behind it? Will it not be certain and inevitable that the soul which is always bathed in such atmosphere, confronted with such ideals, will be-come slovenly, careless, mercenary and selfish? And when some great occasion arises it will call in vain for the high qualities of a noble nature.

Suppose, on the other hand, that we do the little duties of life faithfully, punctually, thoughtfully, re-verently—not for the praise of man, but for the "Well done" of Christ—not for the payment we may receive, but because God has given us a little piece of work to do in His great world—not because we must, but because we choose—not as the slaves of circumstances, but as Christ's freed ones—then far down beneath the surge of common life the foundations of a character are laid, more beautiful and enduring than coral, which shall presently rear itself before the eyes of men and angels, and become an emerald islet, green with perennial beauty, and vocal with the songs of Paradise.

We ought, therefore, to be very careful how we fulfil the common tasks of daily life. We are making the character in which we have to spend eternity. We are either building into ourselves wood, hay, and stubble, which will have to be burnt out at great cost, or the gold, silver, and precious stones that shall be things of beauty and joy for ever.

3. *The Great Doing of Little Things will make a Great Life.*—Let it be granted that you are a person of ordinary ability. It is as likely as not that you will never be removed into a wider sphere than the obscure one in which you have been pining, like a wood-bird in its cage. Give up your useless regret, your querulous complaint, and begin to meet the call of trivial common-place with tenderness to each person you encounter; with faith in God, as doing His best for you; with heroic courage and unswerving fidelity; with patience, thoroughness, submission.

Go on acting thus, week in and week out, year by year, with no thought of human notice, determined always to be at your best, eager only to pay out, without stint, the gold of a noble, unselfish heart. And at the end of life, though you wist not that your face glistens, others will see you shining like the sun in your Heavenly Father's kingdom. It will be discovered that you have unwittingly lived a great life, and you will be greeted on the theshold of heaven with the "Well done" of your Lord.

Some who are sighing for a great life are unconsciously living it in the eye of God's angels. Those who forgo marriage that they may bring up and educate the younger children of their homes; those who deny themselves almost the necessaries of life to add some coals of comfort to the meagre fire at which the chill hands of age warm themselves; those who are not only themselves pure amid temptation, but the centers of purity, shielding others; those who stand to their post of duty though the fires, as they creep near, are scorching the skin and consuming the heart; those who meet the incessant demand of monotonous tasks with gentleness, unselfishness, and the wealth of a strong, true heart—these, though they know not, are graduating for the front rank of heaven's nobility.

> *"Oh! where is the sea?" the fishes cried,*
>   *As they swam the crystal clearness through:*
> *"We've heard from of old of the ocean's tide,*
>   *And so long to look on the waters blue.*
> *The wise ones speak of the infinite sea;*
> *Oh! who can tell us if such there be?"*
>
> *The lark flew up in the morning bright,*
>   *And sang and balanced on sunny wings;*
> *And this was its song: "I see the light,*
>   *I look o'er the world of beautiful things;*
> *But flying and singing everywhere,*
> *In vain I have searched to find the air."*

4. *It is a Greater thing to do Little Things Well than those which seem more Important.*—They who daily handle matters which bulk largely before the eyes of their fellows are expected to act from great motives, and to behave worthily of their great and important position. The statesman is expected to be high-minded, the Christian lady to be virtuous, the minister to be earnest. There is no special credit to any of these for being what they profess, and are expected to be. The current is with them; their difficulty would be to face it.

But surely, in God's sight, it is a much greater thing when the soul conquers adverse circumstances and rises superior to the drift of its associations. To be high-minded when your companions are mean and degraded; to be chaste, when ease and wealth beckon you to enter the gate of vice; to be devout or zealous when no one expects it; to do small things from great motives—this is the loftiest attainment of the soul.

It is a greater thing to do an unimportant thing from a great motive, for God, for truth, for others, than to do an important one; greater to suffer patiently each day a thousand stings than die once as a martyr at the stake. And therefore an obscure life really offers more opportunities for the nurture of the loftiest type of character just because it is less liable to be visited by those meaner considerations of notoriety, or applause, or money, which intrude themselves into more prominent positions, and scatter their deadly taint.

5. *Little Things greatly done prepare for the Right Doing of Great Things.*—We sometimes lay down the story-book or the history with a groan. We had been reading of some sudden opportunity which came to a Grace Darling, reared in the obscurity of a fisherman's home, or to a Florence Nightingale, or a John Brown, living apart from the great world in the heart of the Adirondacks. "Oh," we say, "if only such a chance would dip down into my life and lift me out of it! I'm weary, weary of this dull level." Ah! it is a common mistake. Men think that the occasion makes the hero, whereas it only reveals him.

The train must have been laid long before, and carefully, else the falling of a single spark would never blast the mighty rocks, or shiver the frowning fortress-walls. There must be the fabric of strong and noble character, built up by patient continuance in well-doing, else the sudden appeal of the critical hour will knock vainly at the door of life, and the soul will crouch unanswering and helpless within.

If great opportunities were to come to most, we could make nothing of them. They would pass by us unnoticed or unimproved. They would go from us to those who had more nerve, or gift, or spiritual power than we. You cannot, just because you will, speak a foreign language, or dash off a brilliant air upon the piano, or talk easily on the motive of one of Browning's poems. All these demand long and arduous study: that must be given first in the chamber; and then, if a sudden summons comes for any of them, on the housetop of observation you will be ready.

You cannot be brave in a crisis if you are habitually a coward. You cannot be generous with a fortune, if you are a miser with half-pence. You cannot be unselfish in some such accident which imperils life if you are always

30

"*Again and again*"

pressing for the one vacant seat in train or omnibus, and elbowing your way to the front on every possible occasion. David must practice with sling and stone through long hours in the wilderness, or he will never bring down Goliath. Joseph must be pure in thought, and strong in private self-discipline, or he will never resist the solicitations of the temptress. The Sunday School teacher must be regular, painstaking, faithful in the conduct of his class of little ragged boys, or he will never be promoted to serve his Master as a minister at home, or as a missionary abroad.

6. *Our Behavior in Little Things is the Truest Test of What we are.*—If I were eager to secure a good employee for a responsible position, I should not attach much importance to the way in which the candidate acted on a set occasion, when he knew that he was being observed. Of course he would be on his best behaviour. But give me a private window so that I can watch him in his least considered actions,—how he behaves at home, how he treats his mother and sisters, how he fulfils the common duties of life. What he is then, he is really.

I once recommended a girl as wife to a working-man, because early one morning I came on her unexpectedly in the midst of soap-suds, cheerfully doing the work of her father's home. I knew that a good working-man's daughter would make a good working-man's wife. And the marriage turned out as I expected.

But if this is man's way, may it not be God's? There are great tasks to be fulfilled in eternity: angels to be judged, cities to be ruled; perhaps worlds to be evangelized. For these suitable agents will be required: those who can rule, because they have served; those who can command, because they have obeyed; those who can save others, because they never saved themselves. Perhaps, even now our Heavenly Father is engaged in seeking those among us who can fill these posts. And He is seeking them, not amongst such as are filling high positions in the eyes of men, but in the ranks of such as are treading the trivial round and fulfilling the common task.

From the nearest fixed star, the inequalities of our earth, whether of Alp or molehill, are alike insignificant. We need to look at our positions from the standpoint of eternity, and probably we shall be startled at the small differences between the lots of men. The one thing for us all is to abide in our calling with God, to count ourselves as His fellow-workers, to do what we can in His grace, and for His glory; never excusing ourselves; never condoning failure or misdoing; never content unless, by the help of the Blessed Spirit, we have wrought out His promptings and suggestions to the best of our power, whether in the gold of the extraordinary, or the bronze of the cheaper and more ordinary, achievement.

Of course there is no saving merit in what we do. Salvation is only by simple trust in our Saviour, Jesus. But when we are saved, it gives new zest to Life to do all for Him, as Lord and Master, and to know that He is well pleased in the right-doing of the most trivial duties of the home or daily business (I Peter ii. 20).

May each reader learn this happy art, and go through life offering all to God, as the white-stoled priests in the Temple of old, for indeed, all believers have been made priests unto God: every sphere may be a Holy Temple, and every act, done in the name of Jesus, may be a spiritual sacrifice, acceptable to God through Jesus Christ.

There are fewer differences in our several lots than we are apt to think. Beneath the play of varying circumstances are the same yearnings, sorrows, disappointments, hopes and fears. We learn off the same lesson-books, though for some they are bound in velvet, for others, in cloth boards. But every life may become great, if lived for the great God, and beneath the sway of a great resolve.

WHAT WAS PAUL'S SECRET?

"Now I exhort you to be of good cheer: for there shall be no loss of any man's life among you, but of the ship. For there stood by me this night the angel of God, whose I am, and whom I serve."—ACTS 27:22, 23

PAUL THE APOSTLE was a seafaring man. Before this shipwreck, he had been shipwrecked three times over, and had spent a day and a night lashed to a spar, rising and falling with the billows. So when this was a question whether they should stay in the haven or leave it, his opinion amounted to a good deal. But the centurion who was there with his soldiers carrying the prisoners to Rome, and who was the most important person on board, took more notice of what the captain and the owner of the ship said than of Paul's words. The consequence was, that in spite of all he could say or do, the ship's crew came into imminent danger. I would like you to try and imagine the state of things on the fourteenth night after they had left Crete. The ship was creaking and straining in every timber; the wind was screaming and howling through what cordage there was left, the great waves struck the vessel with a boom of thunder, and to many it must have seemed that the whole ship must go to pieces, and every soul on board meet a watery grave. They had been without food, without regular meals, they were drenched with rain, they were overtired, they were full of dread, and it seemed as though heaven was closed above them, for neither sun, nor moon, nor stars had been visible for many a long day and night.

It was at this time that Paul stood forward and became the true captain of the vessel, the true manager and guide of the whole crew. He had come on board as a prisoner, he was fastened to a soldier, and all through those dark days he had been held fast by an iron fetter to a Roman guard exchanged every four hours; I suppose, indeed, many of the crew would have stood apart from him and avoided him as perhaps a murderer or a felon of some kind. But in the midst of the agony of that fortnight the man's true royalty had begun to show itself. The centurion, the soldiers, the owner, the crew, and the other prisoners all came to feel that this was a kingly man, a real man, a man who was made to command, made for the hour of crisis. It is very wonderful how quiet and calm he was.

There are three indications of it.

The first was that he was able to sleep.

He dreamt of angels, and slept as quietly, and sweetly, and soundly as he would have done had he been in the home of friends. He knew well that God was right. It is indeed a happy thing when a man's heart is so quiet in the midst of a storm that he can find rest.

Then, secondly, he was able to recall the Lord's Supper in that moment. This would not strike you when reading the Bible in English, but in the Greek the word Eucharist is used—he gave thanks. The very word which is used of Christ when He took the bread, blessed, and broke it, is used of Paul when he took some of the ship biscuit soaked with salt water, and began to break it before the people, to eat it himself and share it out. All stood around; there was the centurion, the captain, the owner, the sailors, and the prisoners—two hundred and seventy-six of them gathered together in the great hold of the vessel, from which they had put out the corn; Paul stood in the midst of them; and getting one hand free from the iron, he broke the biscuit as well as he might, looked up to God and gave Him thanks, then passed it round—an action which seemed as if Paul celebrated the Lord's Supper in the midst of that storm and the darkness on board the ship. It showed that his heart was rooted in God for him to be so calm and glad in such an hour as that.

Then the third symptom of the quietness of his soul is given to us in the fact that when there was great confusion on board, and it seemed as if there was to be a rush to the boat, it was Paul who came to the front, told the centurion of the danger, then put the men into such good spirit that the whole crew got safely to shore. All this shows what a cool, quiet, calm heart the man had.

There are many storms that sweep your life. It may be that years ago you left the harbor of your home, the fair haven of your father's house, to venture forth upon life's stormy sea, and the south wind blew softly, and you thought that life was to be merry and happy. But, oh, you know how after that the north wind of trouble and sorrow swept down upon your life, driving you out to sea, and you have been running before the wind these many years, and this house of prayer has been your little island of Crete where you have obtained a brief spell of rest, now and then, till the storm has broken upon you again.

Well, I want to tell you that in that storm that sweeps your life you, too, may have the quiet heart, the sleep and dream of angels; you, too, as you break your crust of bread may find it to be a Eucharist, a Lord's Supper, and you in the midst of some crisis may stand in the front and show yourself to be a leader of men, because you yourself are led of God, and you have learned to pillow your head upon His heart. God help us, then, to learn Paul's secret.

Now what was Paul's secret that made him so calm in

the storm? First, he recognizes God's ownership in "Whose I am." He looked on the storm, and he said, "This is my Father's world; this dark night, it is my Father's; and I am His child, and He loves me too well to forget me. I am His. The God who made this foaming ocean is my Father; the God who lets those winds blow forth is my God; all this world is but a mansion—in my Father's house; and I am safe because my Father rules the storm. 'Whose I am.' I am His because He bought me with the priceless blood of His Son, and if He paid down the ransomed price out of His own dear heart, is He likely to forget me now I am in peril? He brought me to Himself by His Spirit, has married me to Him by eternal and indissoluble bonds, and is He likely to forget the soul that He has taken to be His own? I bear upon my heart the stamp, the mint-mark of His ownership, the brand-mark of my Master, and is it impossible He should forget me? The darkness cannot hide me from Him, and the storm cannot drown my voice."

You, my friend, are His, I trust. You are His sheep, though you may have wandered; you are His coin, bearing His mint-mark, though it has been defaced by many things. You are His child, although perhaps in the far country. But I pray God you may say, "I am His because He made me; I am His because He redeemed me; I am His because He won me; I am His because I have come back to His arms; and wherever I am God will care for me."

The second part of Paul's secret was that he knew he was doing his duty. He was on his way to Rome. He had been brought up in the provinces, so to speak, and had often wanted to go to Rome. He thought if he could get to Rome he would be able to teach the whole world, because Rome was the metropolis of the world. He had even prayed that God would take him there. But God

40

sometimes answers our prayers in a queer fashion. Paul never thought of getting to Rome tied to a jailer on a creaking corn-ship that seemed likely to go to the bottom. When we ask God for anything He often sends the answer in a different way from what we expected. I have lived long enough to know that, though the packing-case may be rough, there is always something good inside. So it was with this answer. God said, "Yes, Paul, I have heard your prayer; you wish to go to Rome; I will send you—carriage paid; you shall have a trip there for nothing; the Roman Emperor shall pay all." That was the way God answered his prayer. He knew he was on the path of duty, that God had just marked out his course; that if the pathway of his life left the sunny upland and dipped down into the dark valley, it was still his Father's, because it was the path his Father chose, and he knew God could make no mistake.

So it is with all of us in life. The one thing that brings comfort to a man's heart is to know that he is just on the path of duty where God put him, and that if danger, and peril, and scorn meet him there, God, who sent him, must take the responsibility. When God sends His servants upon His errands He takes all risks, and when you are doing God's work—then, let the storm come, God is responsible for carrying you there, and you may sleep in the midst of it like Paul himself.

The third part of Paul's secret was that he was a man of prayer, for the text says that God granted him all the crew. "Why," the centurion must have said to himself, "I never saw a man like that before; he never swears, and is always praying; when other prisoners pray they generally put a God before them; but as for this man he does not seem to have a God as far as we can see." There he

41

was morning and night, pleading with God: "My Father, spare these poor soldiers and sailors; they don't know what they do, they don't know Thee; they cannot pray themselves; but I pray for them. Spare their lives for thy dear Son's sake." I speak feelingly of this; for I prayed thus once when crossing the Atlantic in one of those big liners on a night of awful storm. I had crossed the Atlantic some five times, but never in a storm like that. It seemed every moment as if the mighty Atlantic waves were booming, booming, booming against the ship, making her shiver from stem to stern. There, in my cabin—my stateroom—I thought of sailors exposed to the storm whilst we were comparatively so comfortable within. I could not sleep, and instead got down on my knees, and for the first time in my life I spent the whole night on my knees in prayer. It seemed as if God came to me and said: "You must pray; I can trust you to pray; go on praying; and by your prayers you shall win the safety of the vessel and crew." As day broke I was very tired but I felt a cessation of the storm, and I knew in my heart that God had answered my prayer, and all would be well. Now I say when a man gets hold of God in prayer, and wins from Him an answer, that man may have been kept awake a few watches; but after a while he falls asleep soundly in the midst of the storm.

Mr. Moody was in just such another storm, and in the midst of it went and spoke to all the passengers gathered together in the saloon, prayed with them; and then went back to his own stateroom, and fell into the sweetest sleep; and during that sleep they saw a distant vessel that came to their relief. Prayer gives heart's-ease. What will not prayer do on land? what will it not do at sea? "I have given thee the ship, and all that sailed with thee."

That is the third part of the secret. I think, fourthly, that heaven was near to him. "An angel said to me." I believe that sailors sometimes talk about the little cherub that sits up aloft and cares for poor Jack! But thank God His angels don't merely sit up aloft; they come down on the ship. That is what this angel did. "There stood by me an angel of God." I do not care for angels up in heaven, or for angels on "the edge of the storm." I like angels down in the storm, alongside. And that is the way this angel stood near.

You know, of course, of Jacob's ladder, how the angels came down and went up it, and it seemed to that lonely man as if that bit of bleak moorland was as near to heaven as his own father's house which he had left. But, after all, it is not so wonderful to think of God coming down to moorland, because it seems as if that calm country should be linked to God, but it seems very different that God's angels should find their way to an old, creaking corn-ship in the midst of the storm. I believe that angel came straight to the ship in which Paul was. He knew where it was, and he came straight to it, and stood beside him. The fact is that when a man is in the center of God, he has got the circumference of God all round, and when you have God in the heart, you have God's angels around to minister to you. There is no storm so thick that the angels cannot see you, and no wind can blow them out of their course, and no peril in which they cannot help. But oh if it should be God's will for you to go down as many have gone down before you at sea, then the angels are there also to bear you to the bosom of Christ, and the way to heaven is as quick from the ocean as it is from the little village where you first saw the peep of day.

I think the last and the best secret that Paul had was a

good conscience. He and his conscience were able to look each other in the face. The word conscience is Latin, and means to know yourself. It is you and your better self knowing each other, and the man who is right with his better self is a happy man, and the man who is wrong with his better self is a miserable man. I say that man is right with God and man and himself; he is a man who could sleep in the midst of a storm, having exercised himself to have a conscience void of offense before God and before man.

I pray that you may carry through the storm a good conscience with a sense that God is near. Then, though you have only a ship biscuit, it will be like a sacrament, and out of that storm will rise up the constant prayer of your faith to the Almighty.

HOW TO EXPERIENCE PERFECT PEACE

"Thou wilt keep him in perfect peace, whose mind is stayed on thee: because he trusteth in thee."

ISAIAH 26:3

"PEACE, PERFECT PEACE!" What music there is in these words! The very mention of them fills the heart with longings, which cry out for satisfaction, and will not be comforted. Sometimes, indeed, we may succeed in hushing them for a little, as a mother does a fretful child; but soon they will break out again with bitter and insatiable desire. Our nature sighs for rest, as the ocean shell when placed to the ear, seems to sigh for the untroubled depths of its native home.

There is peace in those silent depths of space, blue for very distance, which bend with such gentle tenderness over our fevered, troubled lives. There is peace in the repose of the unruffled waters of the mountain lake, sheltered from the winds by the giant cliffs around. There is peace at the heart of the whirlwind, which sweeps across the desert waste in whirling fury. The peace of a woodland dell, of a highland glen, of a summer landscape, all touch us. And is there none for us, whose nature is so vast, so composite, so wonderful?

There is. As Jacob lay a-dying in his hieroglyphed chamber, not far from the Pyramids, his face shadowed by approaching death, but aglow with the light of the world to which he was going, he told how Shiloh, the Peaceful One, the Peace-giver, should come to give peace to men. Weary generations passed by and still he came not, until at length there stood among men One, whose outward life was full of sorrow and toil; but whose sweet calm face mirrored the unbroken peace that reigned

47

within His breast. He was the promised Peace-giver. He had peace in Himself; for He said, "My peace." He had the power of passing that peace on to others; for He said, "My peace I *give* unto you." Why should not each reader of these lines receive the peace which Jesus had Himself, and which He waits to give to every longing and recipient heart?

A poor woman timidly asked the gardener of a gentleman's hothouse, if he would sell her *just one bunch of grapes for her dying child*. He gruffly threatened to summon the police, unless she quickly left the place. But as she sadly turned away, she was recalled by a girlish voice, bidding her stay, asking her story, and insisting on her having as many bunches as she could carry with her. And when she offered her few half-pence in return, she was met by the sweet, laughing answer, "Nay, my poor woman, this is my father's hothouse; we don't sell grapes here, but we are very pleased to *give* them; take them and welcome, for your dying child." It is so that Jesus *gives* His peace to all weary tired ones. Why not to you?

His peace is *perfect* (Isa. 26:3). Unbroken by storms. Uninvaded by the rabble rout of care. Unreached by the highest surges of sorrow. Unstained by the contaminating touch of sin. The very same peace that reigns in Heaven, where all is perfect and complete.

His peace is *as a river* (Isa. 48:18). The dweller on its banks, in time of drought, is well supplied with water. It is flowing at early dawn, as he goes to his daily toil. It is there in the scorching noon. It is there when the stars shine, hushing him to sleep with the melody of its waves. When he was a child, he plucked the flowerets on its banks; and when his foot shall tread its banks nevermore, his children's children shall come to drink its streams. Think, too, how it broadens and deepens and fills up, in its onward journey, and from its source to the bound-less, infinite sea. So may our peace be, abiding and growing with our years.

His peace is *great* (Isa. 54:13). The mountains may depart and the hills be removed, yet shall it abide. Its music is louder than the tumult of the storm. Learn the lesson of the Lake of Galilee; that the peace which is in the heart of Jesus, and which He gives to His own, can quell the greatest hurricane that ever swept down the mountain ravine and spent itself on the writhing waters beneath. For when the Master arose and rebuked the wind and said unto the sea, "Peace, be still," the winds ceased and there was a great calm. "Great peace have they which love Thy law, and nothing shall offend them."

His peace is *compatible with much tribulation* (John 16:33). If we never find our path dipping down into the sunless valley, we may seriously question whether we have not missed our way to the Celestial City. The road to the Mount of Ascension invariably passes through the shadowed Garden of Gethsemane, and over the steep ascent of Calvary, and then down into the Garden of the Grave. "We must, through much tribulation, enter the Kingdom of God." But amidst it all, it is possible to be kept in unbroken peace, like that which possessed the heart of Jesus, enabling Him calmly to work a miracle of healing amid the tumult of His arrest.

His peace *passeth all understanding* (Phil. 4:7). It cannot be put into words. It defies analysis. It must be felt to be understood. The thing most like it is the gladsomeness of a child in its father's home, where wealth and love and wise nurture combine to supply all its need; but even that falls short of the glorious reality. "Eye hath not seen, nor ear heard, neither have entered into the heart of man, the things which God hath prepared for them that love Him; but God hath revealed them unto us by His Spirit. We have the mind of Christ." And (bringing out the deep meaning of the Greek), we may say, that this peace will *sentinel* our hearts and minds, going to and fro, like a sentry before a palace, to keep off the intruders that would break in upon the sacred enclosure. Oh that we might be ever protected by a guardianship, so benign and watchful and invulnerable to attack.

There are a few conditions, however, which demand our careful thought.

1.—THE BASIS OF PEACE IS THE BLOOD.

"He made peace by the Blood of His Cross" (Col. 1: 20). We sometimes hear men speak of *making their peace with God*. But that is wholly needless. Peace has been made. When Jesus died on the Cross, He did all that needed to be done, and all that could be done, so far as God was concerned, in order to bring peace to men. Nothing more is requisite, save to lay aside fear and suspicion, and to accept the peace which He now sweetly and freely offers. "God was in Christ, reconciling the world unto Himself, not imputing their trespasses unto them . . . now be ye reconciled" (2 Cor. 5: 19-20).

There were many obstacles to our peace, but they have been entirely met, and put out of the way. God's Holy Justice, which would pursue us with its drawn sword, can say nothing against us, because it has been more vindicated in the death of the Son of God, than it could have been in the perdition of myriads of worlds. The broken law, which might press its claims, is silenced by the full and complete satisfaction rendered it in the obedience and death of the Law-giver Himself. Conscience even, with its long and bitter record of repeated sin, feels able to appropriate forgiveness without scruple

50

or alarm; because it understands that God can be just, and yet justify the believer in Jesus. "Who is he that condemneth? It is Christ that died; yea, rather that is risen again; who is even at the right hand of God; who also maketh intercession for us."

On the evening of His resurrection, our Lord entered through the unopened doors into the chamber where His disciples were cowering for fear of the Jews. His benediction, *Peace be unto you*, fell on their ears like the chime of bells amid the storm of Friburg's organ. But He did not rest satisfied with this. Indeed, His words alone would have been in vain. But when He had so said, He showed unto them His hands and His side, fresh from the Cross, with the marks of spear and nails, so that He stood amid them like a lamb, "as it had been slain." Do you wonder that they were glad? The heart must always be glad when it learns the sure basis of Peace in the Blood shed on the Cross. Rest on that precious Blood; make much of it; remember that God sees it, even if you do not; be sure that it pleads through the ages, with undiminished efficacy; and be at peace.

2.—THE METHOD OF PEACE IS BY FAITH IN GOD'S WORD. How many Christians miss God's peace because they look into their hearts to see how they feel. If they feel right and happy they are at peace. But if mists veil the inner sky, or the body is out of health, or the temperature of the heart is low, they become sad and depressed, and ill at ease. Peace has taken its flight. This will never do. Life is one long torture thus. This is not the blessed life which Jesus came to give us. To live like this is indeed to miss the prize of our high calling and to cast discredit on His dear Name. *If you seek peace through the medium of feeling you will seek it in vain.* It may come as a wayfaring man for a night, but it will not tarry.

51

It may visit you like a transient gleam over the hillside, but it will be only a tiny break between long leagues of cloud. There is a more excellent way. Take up the Bible, the Word of God *to you*. Turn to some of the texts, which shine in its firmament, as stars of the first magnitude in the midnight sky. Consider, for instance words like these. Ponder them well. Seek not for frames, or feelings, or even for faith, but concentrate your mind and heart upon their mighty meaning.

"Whosoever *believeth* in Him, shall not perish, but have everlasting life" (John 3:16).

"He that *heareth* My word, and *believeth* on Him that sent Me, hath everlasting life, and shall not come into condemnation, but is passed from death unto life" (John 5:24).

"By Him, *all that believe* are justified from all things" (Acts 13:30).

"The blood of Jesus Christ cleanseth from *all* sin" (1 John 1:7).

What do these words mean? Can they mean one straw less than they say? And if they are as they seem, is it not clear, that directly you *believe*, you stand before God as a reconciled, accepted, and beloved child?

What is it to believe? It is to look up to Jesus, as a personal Saviour, handing over to Him the whole burden of your soul, for time and eternity; sure that He takes what you give, at the moment of your giving it, even though you feel no immediate peace or joy. Belief in the outset is *trust*.

"Your faith is so weak." But that does not matter, because there is not a word said about the amount of faith. The greatest faith could not make you more secure. The smallest faith cannot put you outside the circle of blessing; because the word, *believeth*, is so delightfully vague.

Faith as a grain of mustard seed can move a mountain equally with faith as a walnut-shell. Faith that can only touch the garment hem gets a blessing which those who press may lose.

"You are not sure if you have the right faith." But all faith, any faith, is the right faith. There are not many sorts of faith. The faith that can only lay down its weary weight on Jesus; the faith that *tries* to look to Him; the faith that staggers towards Him and drops into His arms; the faith that cannot cling because its hands are so weak, but which calls to Him, believing that He can save,—*That* is all the faith you need, and having it you are saved.

"But you do not feel saved." And who said that that was an essential condition of salvation? Remember that it is one thing to be saved, and quite another to feel it. The one may exist without the other; and there are no doubt very many, who are certainly the children of God, but who have never had the sweet assurance of salvation, which is the seal of the Spirit, the blossom of grace, the kiss of God. *Directly you look to Jesus, you are saved, whether you feel it or not.* Don't think about your feelings; don't think about your faith; look to Jesus; and reckon that God will keep His word, and save you.

The result of all this must inevitably be peace. Let Satan from without join with the timid heart within in threatening disaster; faith simply turns to the Word of God, and putting its finger on one of His exceeding great and precious promises, replies, "This must fail, ere I can perish; but I know whom I have believed, and am persuaded He will keep His word, and that He is able to keep that which I have committed unto Him."

3.—THE SECRET OF PEACE IS THE CONSTANT REFERENCE OF ALL TO THE CARE OF GOD. "Be anxious in nothing; but in everything by prayer and supplication with thanksgiving let your requests be made known unto God; and the peace of God shall guard your hearts and your thoughts in Christ Jesus" (Phil. 4:6–7). Acid dropped on steel, and allowed to remain there, will soon corrode it. And if we allow worries, anxieties, careworn questioning to brood in our hearts, they will soon break up our peace, as swarms of tiny gnats will make a paradise uninhabitable.

There is only one thing that we can do. We must hand them over to Jesus just as they occur. It will not do to wait until the day is done, but in the midst of its busy rush, whenever we are conscious of having lost our peace, we should stand still and ask the cause, and then lift up our hearts, and pass it off into the care of our loving and compassionate Lord. " 'Tis enough that He should care, why should we the burden bear?"

Ah, what would not our days become, if only we could acquire that blessed habit? We look so weighted, and lead such burdened lives, because we do not trust Jesus with all the little worries of daily life. There is nothing small to Him if it hinders our peace. And when once you have handed aught to him, refuse to take it back again, and treat the tendency to do so as a temptation to which you dare not give way, no, not for a moment.

Care comes from many sources. Our daily food, our dear ones, our worldly prospects, our Christian work, our pathway in life, our growth in the Divine Life—all these contribute their quota to the total sum. Let us take them all, and lay them down at Jesus' feet, and leave them there; and then live looking to Him to do in us, with us, through us, for us, just as He will. And as we give Him our cares, He will give us His peace, and as He does so He will whisper, "My peace I give unto you, let

54

not your heart be troubled, neither let it be afraid."

There is a remarkable text in Isaiah, which teaches us that the Government should be upon the shoulders of Jesus Christ; and that when it is so, there is no end to the increase of Peace. *"Of the increase of His government and peace there shall be no end"* (9:7). Surely these glorious words refer, not only to the government of a nation, but of each individual life also, and they are very searching.

Where is the government of our lives? Is it in our own hands? Then we must not be surprised, if our hearts are like the troubled sea, when it cannot rest. We are out of harmony with God, and with His will, which must be done whether in us or in spite of us. There can be no Peace, because there is perpetual clashing, and rebellion.

But directly we put the government of our lives, down to their smallest details, into the hands of the Lord Jesus; then we enter into His own infinite Peace. And as His government is extended over our hearts and lives, so does our Peace extend, as when the blessed light of dawn spreads like a benediction through the world.

"In Me ye shall have peace." 'Twas our Saviour who said those words. Let us abide in Him. Let us live in Him. Let us walk in Him. Let us make of Him the secret place unto which we may continually resort. And as we are joined to Him, in the intimacy of deepest union, the peace that fills His heart, like a Pacific ocean, shall begin to flow into ours, until they are filled with the very fullness of God; and the peace of God, like a dove, with fluttering wings, shall settle down upon our hearts, and make them its home forevermore.

ARE YOU DWELLING IN THE DUST?

"Awake and sing, ye that dwell in dust, for thy dew is as the dew of herbs."

ISAIAH 26:19

IN EARLIER DAYS, you may have been very conscious of the clear shining of God's face. You awoke in the morning and God was there; all day you spent in the spirit of Brother Lawrence, who was accustomed to say that he was nearer to God when he was in the kitchen serving the dishes for his brother monks than he was when at the sacrament of the Lord's Supper; and it is a blessed thing for the soul when it is more conscious of God than it is of the presence or absence of anyone. That was your lot once.

You felt you were Christ's companion; that He was using you, and there was a constant interchange of holy fellowship between Him and you. But for some reason which you cannot understand the morning light has died out of your life, and instead of your sitting with Christ upon the throne, in the conscious enjoyment of fellowship with Him, you have been brought down into the very dust of neglect and foresakenness; and for a long time now you have been saying, "My God, my God! why hast Thou forsaken me?" You cannot imagine why. The probability is, that in your case it is not the result of any sin on your part, or of any neglect of your duties, but because God is desirous of ascertaining whether you love Him for the light of His face or for Himself.

When my grandchildren stay with us, I like to bring them sweets when I return at night, and I am certain to see their faces, and hear their voices, as they are eagerly expecting me. But if I tell them in the morning that I shall not bring them any presents when I return, and if I still find them waiting for me with their little, eager, glancing, dancing eyes and pattering feet down the passage to the door, I say to myself, The children love me not because I bring them anything, but for myself. And remember, my friend, you are passing through this experience, and God has taken you out of the deliciousness of conscious fellowship with Himself, that you may learn to walk not by sight, but by faith. At the same time I deeply sympathize with you that you have lost the light of His face, and that you sit in the dust of forsakenness and apparent neglect.

At one time of your life you may have been very conscious of being able to locate Christ in prayer. Oftentimes we pray, as it were, into the void; while at other times we locate Christ, as we do our friend on the telephone. You say to him, "Are you there?" and you know that your friend is there because he answers you. So there are times in our lives when Christ is so real to us that instead of putting our letters into the post-box we place them in His hand; indeed, we do not need to write at all, because we speak. But those who have learned to speak with Christ feel it very irksome when the months pass and there is no direct contact with His Spirit; when prayers come back to us; or when they are drowned at sea like carrier-pigeons are sometimes; and the letter never gets to its destination, or the letters are returned to us and lie all around like returned letters from the dead-letter office. A life like that, as contrasted with fellowship on the mountain of prayer answered and prayer enjoyed, brings a soul into a consciousness of desertion, and such may be included as one who sits "in the dust."

Are You Dwelling in the Dust?

On the other hand, perhaps your ideals are all behind you. The soul can live so long as its ideals are in front; so long as the Alpine summits beckon us from afar, so long as there is something to realize, something to effect. When the girl stands at the marriage altar with a dream of happy wifehood and motherhood perhaps; or when the young minister stands on the ordination day surrounded by presbyters, to set himself apart for the service of his life-work, there is not a man or woman who does not dream great dreams. So long as ideals go before him no man can really die. I believe some men and women are kept alive by ideals; but it is a sad thing when you meet a woman in middle life who has got that look of disappointment; many a young girl who bade fair to be a saint gets coarsened, I think it is partly because she has been disappointed, and her ideals are not realized, and she has allowed herself to drift. I hope no woman here will ever allow herself to lose her ideals, even though she meets with resistance and disappointment; still dress your sweetest, look your nicest, and care for the home, making it as happy as possible, though your heart is like lead within you. In middle life and afterwards we get beyond our ideals. They are like the withered flowers of a bridal bouquet—a handful of withered leaves. The heart that sits alone, when the light of some great hope has passed, may well be said to sit "in the dust."

You may be one who has committed some sin, a sin probably that was not meant to be a sin, but was committed in hours of weakness; for the longer I live in the world the more I see that people are but seldom intentionally criminals at the start; most of us are weak, compliant, and complaisant, and we do things and say things almost without knowing it, which drift us into positions from which we cannot extricate ourselves, and then it is we break our wings and cannot rise; then we drop from our aerial flight into the dust. I noticed in *The Westminster Gazette* a review of the life of Rossetti, and it was said that Rossetti never got over his wife's death, because he thought he had not been perfectly kind to her during the last years of her life, and that she might have lived longer if he had been more kindly. His friends repudiate that, and say it is not true; but if it was not true of Rossetti, it is true of many people. The sin of neglect, the sin of inattention, the sin of absorption in self, these have wrought a great sorrow in the lives of some, and they never rise out of the dust after.

Lastly, perhaps you are in very difficult pecuniary circumstances. Men may say what they like about money, but it is very pleasant to have a little of it, especially when life is getting to autumn. One sympathizes profoundly with people who know that soon they will be too old, at forty or fifty, to hold their berth, and who have never been able to save. One feels terribly for families, with heads of which have lost their situations. Winter will soon be upon them, and nothing wherewith to meet it—nothing but the sale of the furniture. One feels deeply for those who once held their heads high, whose children, once educated in expensive schools, have been necessarily withdrawn. One feels deeply for families who have come down in the world so suddenly that they have to look at every penny, and instead of availing themselves of trams or trains, find it necessary to go on foot. These people, with breaking hearts, are described as sitting "in the dust."

I have thus indicated five classes of people, namely: those who think themselves forsaken of God; those who have lost the power of locating Christ in prayer; those whose ideals are behind them and withered, which they cannot alter; and those who are passing through circumstances of poverty, and are suffering from straitened incomes. All these people may be described as having been brought down from the throne to the dust. "Thy dead men shall live, together with my dead body shall they arise. Awake and sing, ye that dwell in dust; for thy dew is as the dew of herbs, and the earth shall cast out her dead."

You may have seen that picture in which hope is depicted as a blindfolded maiden, with downcast face, sitting upon the axis of the earth. Above her shines the morning star, and already the air is blue with translucent light; she, however, sees it not, while the earth is making her difficult progress through a sea of floating cirri. In her left hand she is holding her lyre, every string is broken except one, and she is intently hearkening to its vibration, as though it lay between her and absolute despair.

I say to you, my friend, take these words, and above all, take the thought of the great God, from whom you came and to whom you will go, and let that chord vibrate until the bandage is torn from your eyes and you find yourself bathed in morning light.

"Awake and sing, ye that dwell in the dust." The first thing I notice, and to me it is a great comfort, is that God does not leave us alone. Nothing would be more awful to me than that God should let me be untroubled, untempted, undisturbed, for then I should begin to think that He despaired of making anything of me. If only God will do something; if only He will show me that He thinks it is worth while! Suppose God did not think it worth while to train you, to educate you, to sift you, would that not be the most despairing conception of

God, or of yourself, which could be presented? If God said, "That soul is so worthless, so mean, so trashy, that it is absolutely not worth my while to do anything with it, I will throw it on the scrap-heap." Would not that be a worse condition of things than to be emptied from vessel to vessel, and brought down from the throne to the dust?

I thank God He has never let me alone, and during every six months of my life He has been putting me through discipline, disappointment, suffering, letting me know His cross and passion. I venture to hope that I shall be some good some day, or else He would never have taken all this trouble about me. It is better to be down in the dust than to be up on the throne, and for God to say, "Sit there, man, it is no use your stirring. I can make nothing of you." No, the very fact that God brings you through it all proves that you are not a piece of glass, but that you are a real diamond. If you were a piece of glass, the great lapidary would throw you aside and say, "It is of no use, I can make nothing out of that raw material." But the fact that God has put you on the lapidary's wheel, cutting His facets in you, proves you are a diamond; yet don't be proud, because a diamond is only charcoal, you know!

The second thing that calls for singing is that God is nearer to you, now that you are low, than when you were high. Of course, I am only speaking in the language of men, because God is equally near us always, but when we are in trouble God seems to come nearer to us. In the twenty-third Psalm David sings of the old, far-away days when he was a shepherd-boy. You may be sure that Psalm 23 was written when David was an old man; the lights were getting dim, and he turned back to the days of his boyhood—for we never appreciate our

morning hours till night begins to draw the curtains
You remember he speaks about God in the first three
verses:—

The Lord is my Shepherd; I shall not want.
He maketh me to lie down in green pastures;
He leadeth me beside the still waters.
He restoreth my soul;
He leadeth me in the paths of righteousness
    for His name's sake.

But in the fourth verse, when he begins to descend from
the shining uplands into the dark gorge, where the
fir-trees cast their black shadows, and the murmur of the
torrent is heard in its bed; where the growl of the wild
beast is on the air, making the soul reel with fear, then
he says "Thou." He talks about God when he is in the
light; he talks to God in a whisper when he is in the
dark. And you can always talk best to God when you
are in the dark. It is evident surely to us all that it is the
child who has fallen down and hurt itself in the dust
that the mother expends her pity on; the children who
can run and do for themselves she leaves to themselves;
but if her little crippled child catches its crutch on a stone
and tumbles, you will hear the mother crooning over it,
picking it up, condoling with it, pressing the little crum-
pled body to her heart. Nothing is so terrible to a
mother as when she sees her child, just born into the
world, will have to carry with it something she has
transmitted; and I always think when you and I are
going through the fire, and are sitting in the dust, it
touches God to the quick, and He is nearer to us. Did
He not say once to Israel, "I have made, and I will
bear?"

One day I saw a big blacksmith bend over his little
child in a cot, and the child got his tiny hand entangled
in the blacksmith's long beard. Presently his wife came
in, saying, "Come away to tea." "I cannot," he said, "the
child has fast hold of me." It was quite clear the child
had not got him by the sense of power; but in a way it
had, by its yearning, helpless need. A crippled child will
pull God down out of heaven. You cannot pull God
down when you are rich, and strong and independent;
but you can pull God down to the dust when you lie
there. You have got more of God, now, than you used to
have. God is more real to you, and if you learn nothing
else all this winter except through your weakness to be
borne on the Everlasting Arms of Omnipotence you are
gaining.

Thirdly, don't you see that it is only when you get
down to the dust that God can really manipulate you. I
want to remind you of that text in Genesis where it is
said, "God made man out of the dust." Where shall I lay
the emphasis: "*God* made man out of the dust"; "God
made *man* out of the dust"; or "God made man out of the
dust?" Whichever way you throw the emphasis, it is a
marvellous correlation of words. God could not make man
out of rocks. He could only mould the likeness of the
body out of dust. Why do your children like the sandy
watering-places? They will say of some seaside resorts:
"Don't go there father because of all those pebbles."
What are pebbles? They are dust in the making, but
they would take a lot of grinding in the great machines
of Nature before they became dust. The children love
the sandy shore, because with their little spades they
can scoop the sand, fashion little hills, cause deep impressions; they can make mimic fortresses, castles and

terraces out of sand, and there is no knowing what a child may not make out of sand. God cannot make men and women out of rocks; He has to grind us down to the dust, that He may mould us.

When I was in Kimberley I was taken to the great diamond-mine there, and saw first the blasting of the rocks; then that they took those rocks and laid them out under the sky to be desiccated. And after six months these rocks, full of diamonds, were placed in mighty crushing machines, driven by an engine of 1,000 horse power. This grinding process was intended to rub down the rocks till they became dust. Out of the dust, diamonds were caught on the grease of the pulsating machine, whereas the garnets passed on and were lost. God grinds us to the very dust, because it is only out of the dust He gets His diamonds. Out of the dust He can mould and fashion us.

I remember so well when God first, in my young life, began to deal with me. I thought of it when I was speaking just now to you who are reduced in circumstances. When a boy about fourteen I suddenly learned that my father had lost his money. He had suddenly to pull up his business that he might be able to pay every man his own. This put an end to my prospects; but I knelt down quietly before God and said: "God, you are more than money," and it was then that God began to make me His child. He cannot do much with you when you are rich and strong, full of self-confidence and self-sufficiency; and therefore God brings us down to the dust that He may begin to fashion us into His own image.

There are two reasons more. The dew gathers near the dust. "Thy dew is as the dew of herbs." The dew is of course the blessed emblem of the Holy Spirit as He distils upon the soul. He may be as the rushing mighty wind, or as a great torrent, the river of life proceeding from the throne of God and of the Lamb. There are, however, some souls which cannot stand the rush of the tornado; they are broken and injured by tidal billows of glory and of power; and, just as God baptizes the parched herbage with the gentle sprinkling of the dew drops, He becomes to such as the dew. There are many souls who cannot deal with the Holy Ghost as Elijah did, but yet are subject to Him, as Elisha was; for while the Holy Ghost came to Elijah with the tidal wave of power, He distilled upon Elisha's humble nature as dew. Perhaps you get more of God when you are baptized in God, as with the dew spray in the early morning, than when God is to you as a torrent. "Thy dew is as the dew of herbs." The dew is not found upon the top of the tall poplar, but on the grass. You know how we go forth on a May morning and our boots get wet, and we have to hasten in to change them when we have walked through those dewy pastures so full of the breath of our exquisite May. And so the Holy Spirit is very near you, baptizing you as you yield to Him, saying, "My God, I am willing to be a blade of grass, if Thou wilt give me my own coronet of jewels of the dew."

Don't be afraid of God, my friend. When we send people to the hospital, what do we expect? We expect the surgeon to do all he can; the doctor to do all he can; and the nurse to do all she should. But do we not expect the hospital to keep them in beef tea and other delights? I often feel that that is the best part of the hospital for some of these poor things. We do not expect the surgeon to operate and that there should be no nourishment given. Some of you are so foolish, you think God is going to operate on you, and that life is just one operating chamber; you don't realize that God is going to give you your beef tea. All the time that He is operating upon you He will see that your body is allowed to be nourished. "Poor thing, she could not stand the operation," I have been told; or, "We could not operate upon her until we had built her up a bit." So they build the patients up a bit, and then operate. And depend upon it, if God is educating you for heaven He is not so mean as to do all the surgery, and not to keep you in the meanwhile. God is not like that! He will give you your beef-tea, my friend.

Lastly, we are to "awake and sing," because out of every grave with its dust there is ultimately a resurrection. Even in our common parlance we say, "It is a long lane that has no turning"; and, "Be the day dreary, be the day long; at last it ringeth to evensong." The watcher knows that presently the darkest night will thin into the grey dawn. There is always an end to things. Pain is limited. At last there comes the swooning, when we can suffer no more, and we fall into a gentle sleep, and forget ourselves. There is always a limit, always a "thus far, and no further." Always the resurrection dawn on the third day; always "the earth shall cast out her dead."

One most beautiful illustration of this is given us in the life of Dante. Next to Christ he was, I should think, one of the saddest men that ever walked this earth. You remember he caught sight of a girl's face, and that broke his heart for ever. He never spoke to her; but once I think they touched one another when they were standing out of a rain storm under a common portico. He had only seen her face. She was married to another, and never knew his love. He was afterwards expelled from Florence, and died between forty and fifty, a poor teacher in

Vienna, longing to see again the baptistery where he had been baptized; but was never permitted again to stand in the old cathedral.

But even to that sad life there was a resurrection. He tells us in his first book, he went down into the depths of hell where the intense heat became ice for its very intensity; then he climbed to the lake that lay above—a beautiful, lovely lake, and found himself amid the rushes round its margin, a token of humility. And then began the further climb; and as he climbed the hill of Paradise, half way up, Beatrice met him—because a man always does meet his ideal again. You will see your Beatrice; you will see what you hoped to be; what you had meant to be; what you started out to be and never attained. Beatrice will meet you some day somewhere. And Beatrice took his hand, and led him to the Rose of Paradise, the petals of which are holy souls, and the heart of which is God Himself. That is the conception given in that wonderful poem of the way in which a man or woman comes finally to resurrection.

In you there is the imprisoned angel, in you there is the imprisoned Christ; in you there is the possibility of the royal soul. And though the stone lies upon the grave, it is true "Thy dead men shall live." The fact is Jesus Christ is always going forth to resurrection. I am always hearing Him say, "All Hail!" I am always seeing Him upon the pathway. I am always aware that He is going in front. Again and again He has been buried, by the Pagan Empire in the fourth century, by the Popes before Luther's day; but He is always rising, and at the present day He has risen and calls us to follow Him. We shall realize our ideals, we shall be what we meant to be, we shall arise, as certainly as God is God, and that the day will break tomorrow, and more certainly. Those who have suffered shall reign; those who have fallen into the dust to die shall find their spring and summer and autumn too. Those who have gone down into the grave of Joseph shall wake upon the Easter morning, and they shall follow their ascended Lord beyond the mist and storm into those pure and blessed heights where God is all in all. Then, quit of our mortal coarseness, and delivered from our fear, and reaping the result of all our pains and sorrows, we shall triumph over time and death, and shine in a life which shall climb ever towards its zenith.

WHERE DID I GO WRONG?

"The Lord shall be thine everlasting light, and the days of thy mourning shall be ended."

ISAIAH 60:20

THIS IS YOUR EAGER QUESTION, and your bitter complaint. On the faces and in the lives of others, you have discerned a light, a joy, a power, which you envy. It is well when we are dissatisfied with the low levels on which we have been wont to live, and begin to ask the secret of a sweeter, nobler, more victorious life. The sleeper who turns restlessly is near awaking, and will find that already the light of the morning is shining around the couch on which slumber has been indulged too long. "Awake, thou that sleepest, and arise from the dead, and Christ shall give thee light."

We must, however, remember that *temperaments differ*. Some seem born in the dark, and carry with them through life an hereditary predisposition to melancholy. Their nature is set to a minor key, and responds most easily and naturally to depression. They look always on the dark side of things, and in the bluest of skies discover the cloud no bigger than a man's hand. Theirs is a shadowed pathway, where glints of sunshine strike feebly and with difficulty through the dark foliage above.

Such a temperament may be yours: and if it be, you never can expect to obtain just the same exuberant gladness which comes to others, nor must you complain if it is so. This is the burden which your Saviour's hands shaped for you, and you must carry it for Him, not complaining, or parading it to the gaze of others, or allowing it to master your steadfast and resolute spirit, but bearing it silently, and glorifying God amid all. But, though it may

75

be impossible to win the joyousness which comes to others, there may at least be rest, and victory, and serenity—Heaven's best gift to man.

We must remember, also, that *emotion is no true test of our spiritual state*. Rightness of heart often shows itself in gladness of heart, just as bodily health generally reveals itself in exuberant spirits. But it is not always so. In other words, absence of joy does not always prove that the heart is wrong. It may do so, but certainly not invariably. Perhaps the nervous system may have been overtaxed, as Elijah's was in the wilderness, when, after the long strain of Carmel and his flight was over, he lay down upon the sand and asked to die, a request which God met, not with rebuke, but with food and sleep. Perhaps the Lord has withdrawn the light from the landscape in order to see whether He was loved for Himself or merely for His gifts. Perhaps the discipline of life has culminated in a Gethsemane, where the bitter cup is being placed to the lips by a Father's hand, though only a Judas can be seen, and in the momentary anguish caused by the effort to renounce the will, it is only possible to lie upon the ground, with strong crying and tears, which the night wind bears to God. Under such circumstances as these exuberant joy is out of place. Somber colors become the tried and suffering soul. High spirits would be as unbecoming here as gaiety in the home shadowed by death. Patience, courage, faith are the suitable graces to be manifested at such times.

But, when allowance is made for all these, it is certain that many of us are culpably missing a blessedness which would make us radiant with the light of Paradise; and the loss is attributable to some defect in our character which we shall do well to detect and make right.

76

Where Did I Go Wrong?

1. *Perhaps you do not distinguish between your standing and your experience.*—Our experiences are fickle as April weather; now sunshine, now cloud; lights and shadows chasing each other over miles of heathery moor or foam-flecked sea. But our standing in Jesus changes not. It is like Himself—the same yesterday, to-day, and for ever. It did not originate in us, but in His everlasting love, which, foreseeing all that we should be, loved us notwithstanding all. It has not been purchased by us, but by His precious blood, which pleads for us as mightily and successfully when we can hardly claim it, as when our faith is most buoyant. It is not maintained by us, but by the Holy Spirit. If we have fled to Jesus for salvation, sheltering under Him, relying on Him, and trusting Him, though with many misgivings, as well we may, then we are one with Him for ever. We were one with Him in the grave; one with Him on the Easter morn; one with Him when He sat down at God's right hand. We are one with Him now as He stands in the light of His father's smile, as the limbs of the swimmer are one with the head, though it alone is encircled with the warm glory of the sun, while they are hidden beneath the waves. And no doubt or depression can for a single moment affect or alter our acceptance with God through the blood of Jesus, which is an eternal fact.

You have not realized this, perhaps, but have thought that your standing in Jesus was affected by your change-ful mood. As well might the fortune of a ward in chancery be diminished or increased by the amount of her spending money. Our standing in Jesus is our invested capital, our emotions at the best are but our spending money, which is ever passing through our pocket or purse, never exactly the same. Cease to consider how you feel, and build on the immovable rock of what Jesus is, and has done,

77

and is doing, and will do for you, world without end.

2. *Perhaps you live too much in your feelings, too little in your will.*—We have no direct control over our feelings, but we have over our will. "Our wills are ours, to make them Thine." God does not hold us responsible for what we *feel*, but for what we *will*. In His sight we are not what we feel, but what we will. Let us, therefore, not live in the summer-house of emotion, but in the central citadel of the will, wholly yielded and devoted to the will of God.

At the Table of the Lord the soul is often suffused with holy emotion, the tides rise high, the tumultuous torrents of joy knock loudly against the flood-gates as if to beat them down, and every element in the nature joins in the choral hymn of rapturous praise. But the morrow comes, and life has to be faced in the grimy counting-house, the dingy shop, the noisy factory, the godless workroom; and as the soul compares the joy of yesterday with the difficulty experienced in walking humbly with the Lord, it is inclined to question whether it is quite so devoted and consecrated as it was. But, at such a time, how fair a thing it is to remark that the will has not altered its position by a hair's breadth, and to look up and say, "My God, the springtide of emotion has passed away like a summer brook; but in my heart of hearts, in my will, Thou knowest I am as devoted, as loyal, as desirous to be only for Thee, as in the blessed moment of unbroken retirement at Thy feet." This is an offering with which God is well pleased. And thus we may live a calm, peaceful life.

3. *Perhaps you have disobeyed some clear command.*—Sometimes a soul comes to its spiritual adviser, speaking thus:

"I have no conscious joy, and have had but little for years."

"Did you once have it?"

"Yes, for some time after my conversion to God."

"Are you conscious of having refused obedience to some distinct command which came into your life, but from which you shrank?"

Then the face is cast down, and the eyes film with tears, and the answer comes with difficulty.

"Yes, years ago I used to think that God required a certain thing of me; but I felt I could not do what He wished, was uneasy for some time about it, but after awhile it seemed to fade from my mind, and now it does not often trouble me."

"Ah, soul, that is where thou hast gone wrong, and thou wilt never get right till thou goest right back through the weary years to the point where thou didst drop the thread of obedience, and performest that one thing which God demanded of thee so long ago, but on account of which thou didst leave the narrow track of implicit obedience."

Is not this the cause of depression to thousands of Christian people? They are God's children, but they are disobedient children. The Bible rings with one long demand for obedience. The key-word of the book of Deuteronomy is, *Observe and Do*. The burden of the Farewell Discourse is, *If ye love Me keep My commandments*. We must not question or reply or excuse ourselves. We must not pick and choose our way. We must not take some commands and reject others. We must not think that obedience in other directions will compensate for disobedience in some one particular. God gives one command at a time, borne in upon us, not in one way only, but in many; by this He tests us. If we obey in

79

this, He will flood our soul with blessing, and lead us forward into new paths and pastures. But if we refuse in this, we shall remain stagnant and waterlogged, make no progress in Christian experience, and lack both power and joy.

4. *Perhaps you are permitting some known evil.*—When water is left to stand, the particles of silt betray themselves, as they fall one by one to the bottom. So, if you are quiet, you may become aware of the presence in your soul of permitted evil. Dare to consider it. Do not avoid the sight as the bankrupt avoids his tell-tale ledgers, or as the consumptive patient the stethoscope. Compel yourself quietly to consider whatever evil the Spirit of God discovers to your soul. It may have lurked in the cupboards and cloisters of your being for years, suspected but unjudged. But whatever it be, and whatever its history, be sure that it has brought the shadow over your life which is your daily sorrow.

Does your will refuse to relinquish a practice or habit which is alien to the will of God?

Do you permit some secret sin to have its unhindered way in the house of your life?

Do your affections roam unrestrained after forbidden objects?

Do you cherish any resentment or hatred towards another, to whom you refuse to be reconciled?

Is there some injustice which you refuse to forgive, some charge which you refuse to pay, some wrong which you refuse to confess?

Are you allowing something yourself which you would be the first to condemn in others, but which you argue may be permitted in your own case, because of certain reasons with which you attempt to smother the remonstrances of conscience?

In some cases the hindrance to conscious blessedness lies not in sins, but in *weights* which hang around the soul. Sin is that which is always and everywhere wrong; but a weight is anything which may hinder or impede the Christian life, without being positively sin. And thus a thing may be a weight to one which is not so to another. Each must be fully persuaded in his own mind. And wherever the soul is aware of its life being hindered by the presence of only one thing, then, however harmless in itself, and however innocently permitted by others, there can be no alternative, but it must be cast aside as the garments of the lads when, on the village green, they compete for the prize of the wrestle or the race.

5. *Perhaps you look too much inwards on self, instead of outwards on the Lord Jesus.*—The healthiest people do not think about their health; the weak induce disease by morbid introspection. If you begin to count your heartbeats, you will disturb the rhythmic action of the heart. If you continually imagine a pain anywhere, you will produce it. And there are some true children of God who induce their own darkness by morbid self-scrutiny. They are always going back on themselves, analyzing their motives, re-considering past acts of consecration, comparing themselves with themselves. In one form or another self is the pivot of their life, albeit that it is undoubtedly a religious life. What but darkness can result from such a course? There are certainly times in our lives when we must look within, and judge ourselves, that we may not be judged. But this is only done that we may turn with fuller purpose of heart to the

Lord. And when once done, it needs not to be repeated. "Leaving the things behind" is the only safe motto. The question is, not whether we did as well as we might, but whether we did as well as we could at the time.

We must not spend all our lives in cleaning our windows, or in considering whether they are clean, but in sunning ourselves in God's blessed light. That light will soon show us what still needs to be cleansed away, and will enable us to cleanse it with unerring accuracy. Our Lord Jesus is a perfect reservoir of everything the soul of man requires for a blessed and holy life. To make much of Him, to abide in Him, to draw from Him, to receive each moment from His fulness, is therefore the only condition of soul-health. But to be more concerned with self than with Him, is like spending much time and thought over the senses of the body, and never using them for the purpose of receiving impressions from the world outside. Look off unto Jesus. Delight thyself in the Lord. My soul, wait thou only upon God!

6. *Perhaps you spend too little time in communion with God through His Word.*—It is not necessary to make long prayers, but it is essential to be much alone with God; waiting at His door; hearkening for His voice; lingering in the garden of Scripture for the coming of the Lord God in the dawn or cool of the day. No number of meetings, no fellowship with Christian friends, no amount of Christian activity can compensate for the neglect of the still hour.

When you feel least inclined for it, there is most need to make for your closet with the shut door. Do for duty's sake what you cannot do as a pleasure, and you will find it become delightful. You can better thrive without nourishment than become happy or strong in Christian life without fellowship with God.

When you cannot pray for yourself, begin to pray for others. When your desires flag, take the Bible in hand, and begin to turn each text into petition; or take up the tale of your mercies, and begin to translate each of them into praise. When the Bible itself becomes irksome, inquire whether you have not been spoiling your appetite by sweetmeats and renounce them; and believe that the Word is the wire along which the voice of God will certainly come to you, if the heart is hushed, and the attention fixed. "I will hear what God the Lord shall speak."

More Christians than we can count are suffering from a lack of prayer and Bible study, and no revival is more to be desired than that of systematic private Bible study. There is no short and easy method of godliness which can dispense with this.

Many also suffer from the spirit of organization and routine, which is so rife in Christian work. We do so much; and we do it mechanically. We are wheels in the great machinery, instead of souls, the value of whose work in the world depends much more on what they are than on what they say or do. We must keep fresh, tender, unselfish, and devout. And it were better to relinquish some of the routine of life than lose the temper and tone of heart, which are all important for the redemption of others.

7. *Perhaps you have never given yourself entirely over to the Mastership of the Lord Jesus.*—We are His by many ties and rights. But too few of us recognize His Lordship. We are willing enough to take Him as Saviour; we hesitate to

make Him King. We forget that God has exalted Him to be Prince, as well as Saviour. And the Divine order is irreversible. Those who ignore the Lordship of Jesus cannot build up a strong or happy life.

Put the sun in its central throne, and all the motions of the planets assume a beautiful order. Put Jesus on the throne of the life, and all things fall into harmony and peace. Seek first the kingdom of God, and all things are yours. Consecration is the indispensable condition of blessedness.

So shall light break on thy path, such as has not shone there for many days. Yea, "thy sun shall no more go down, neither shall thy moon withdraw herself; but the Lord shall be unto thee an everlasting light, *and the days of thy mourning shall be ended.*"

FINDING THE LOST CHORD

"And let him return unto the Lord, and he will have mercy upon him; and . . . he will abundantly pardon."

ISAIAH 55:7

THE STORY OF THE LOST CHORD has been told in exquisite verse, and in stately music. We have all heard of the lady, who in the autumn twilight, which softly filled the room, laid her fingers on the open keys of a glorious organ. She knew not what she was playing, or what she was dreaming then; but she struck one chord of music, like the sound of a great amen.

> It flooded the crimson twilight,
>   Like the close of an angel's psalm;
> And it lay on her fevered spirit
>   With a touch of infinite calm.
>
> It quieted pain and sorrow,
>   Like love overcoming strife;
> It seemed the harmonious echo
>   From our discordant life.
>
> It linked all perplexed meanings,
>   Into one perfect peace;
> And trembled away into silence
>   As if it were loth to cease.

Something called her away, and when she returned to the organ, she had lost that chord divine. Though she longed for it, and sought it, it was all in vain. It was a lost chord.

Whenever I hear that story, it reminds me of the lost joy, the lost peace, the lost power, of which so many complain. At the beginning of their Christian life, near at hand, or right back in the past, it would seem as if they had struck the chord of a blessed and glorious life. As long as those notes lingered in their lives, they were like the days of heaven upon earth, but alas! they died away soon into silence—and all their life is now filled with regret for the grace of days that are dead.

> Where is the blessedness I knew
>   When first I saw the Lord?
> Where is the soul-refreshing view
>   Of Jesus and His Word?
>
> What peaceful hours I then enjoyed!
>   How sweet their memory still!
> But they have left an aching void,
>   The world can never fill.

These words are written to help all such and to give them again the sweet lost chord. Take heart! You may again have all, and more than all that you have ever lost. You have flung your precious stones into the deep, there has been a moment's splash, a tiny ripple, and they have sunk down and down, apparently beyond hope of recovery. Yet the hand of Christ will again place them on your palm. Only henceforth, be wise enough to let Him keep them for you.

These are the steps back—steps you may take at once:—

1.—*Be sure that God will give you a hearty Welcome.* He is not an angry Judge. He has not given you up or ceased to love you. He longs after you. His portrait is drawn by One who could not mislead us, who compares Him to the Father of a loved and prodigal boy, ever watching from His windows the road by which the truant went, eagerly longing for his return, and ready, if he should

see him a great way off, to run to meet him, and clasp him,
rags and filth and all, to his yearning heart. That is thy
God, my friend. Listen to His words, broken by sighs,
"How shall I give thee up, Ephraim? how shall I deliver
thee, Israel? how shall I make thee as Admah? how shall
I set thee as Zeboim? Mine heart his turned within Me,
My compassions are kindled." Read the last chapter of
the Book of Hosea, which may be well called the
backsliders' gospel. Read the third chapter of Jeremiah,
and let the plaintive pleadings to return soak into your
spirit. Read the story of Peter's fall and restoration, and
let your tears fall thick and fast on John 21, as you learn
how delicately the Lord forgave, and how generously
He intrusted the backslider with His sheep and lambs.
Be sure that though your repeated failures and sins have
worn out everyone else, they have not exhausted the
infinite love of God. He tells us to forgive our offending
brother unto four hundred and ninety times, how much
oftener will He not forgive us? According to the height
of heaven above the earth, so great is His mercy. "Let
the wicked forsake his way, and the unrighteous man his
thoughts, and let him return unto the Lord, and He will
have mercy upon him, and to our God, for He will
abundantly pardon." If you go back to God, you are
sure of a hearty welcome.

2.—*Seek to know and confess whatever has come between
God and you.* You have lost the light of God's face, not
because He has arbitrarily withdrawn it, but because
your iniquities have come between you and your God,
and your sins, like a cloud before the sun, have hid His
face from you. Do not spend time by looking at them as a
whole, deal with them one by one. The Boer is a formi-
dable foe to the British soldier, because he is trained
from boyhood to take a definite aim and bring down his

mark, while our soldiers fire in volleys. In dealing with sin, we should imitate him in the definiteness and accuracy of his aim. Ask God to search you and show you what wicked way is in you. Marshal all your life before Him, as Joshua marshaled Israel, sift it through, tribe by tribe, family by family, household by household, man by man, until at last you find the Achan who has robbed you of the blessed smile of God. Do not say: Lord, I am a great sinner, I have done what I ought not, I have not done what I ought. But say, Lord, I have sinned in this, and this, and that, and the other. Call up each rebel sin, by its right name, to receive sentence of death. Your heart is choked with sins; empty it out, as you would empty a box, by handing out first the articles that lie on the surface. When you have removed them, you will see more underneath; hand them out also. When these are removed, you will probably see some more. Never rest till all are gone. Confession is just this process of telling God the unvarnished story—the sad, sad story—of each accursed sin. How it began. How you sinfully permitted it to grow. How you have loved and followed it to your bitter cost.

3.—*Believe in God's instant forgiveness.* How long does it take you to forgive your child, when you are sure that it is really sorry and repentant? Time is not considered in forgiveness. The estrangement of a lifetime, the wrongdoing of years may be forgiven in the twinkling of an eye, in the time that a tear takes to form and fall. So it is with God. If we confess our sins, He is faithful and just to forgive us. He does sometimes keep us waiting for an answer to other prayers, but He never keeps us waiting one single second for an answer to our prayer for forgiveness. It is hardly possible for the prodigal to stammer out the words: Father, I have sinned, before the answer flashes upon him, I have put away thy sin, thou shalt not die. There is not a moment's interval between the humble and sad telling of the story of sin and God's forgiveness. As soon as a penitent appears in the doorway of God's throne-room, the golden scepter of His royal forgiveness is stretched out for him to touch. You may not feel forgiven. You may have no ecstasy of joy. But you are forgiven, in the thoughts of God. The angels hear Him say: *Child, thy sins, which are many, are all forgiven thee; go in peace.* If we confess, and as soon as we confess, He is faithful and just to forgive. He never says, Go thy way, and return tomorrow, and I will see whether I can forgive. He hates the sin, and is only too glad to sweep it away. He loves the sinner, and is only too happy to receive him again to His embrace. And He is able to do all this so quickly and so entirely, because Jesus Christ our Lord bare our sins in His own body on the tree.

4.—*Give up the cause of past failure.* True repentance shows itself in eager care not to offend again. This care prompts the sinner to go back on his past life to discover how it was that he came to sin, and to avoid the cause. Is it a friendship? Then he will cut the tender cord, though it were the thread of his life. Is it an amusement? Then he will forever absent himself from that place, those scenes, and that companionship. Is it a profitable means of making money? Then he will rather live on a crust than follow it a moment longer. Is it a study, a pursuit, a book? Then he will rather lose hand, or foot, or eye, than miss the favor of God, which is life. Is it something that the Church permits? Nevertheless, to him it shall be sin. If you cannot walk on ice without slipping or falling, it is better to not go on at all. If you cannot digest certain food, it is better not to put it in the mouth.

It may seem impossible to extricate yourself from certain entanglements which have woven themselves about you. Nevertheless, remember Him who said, Let My people go, that they may serve Me. He cut the knot for them; if you trust Him, He will cut it for you. Or if He does not cut it at a single blow, He will untie it by the patient workings of His Providence.

5.—*Take any public step that may be necessary.* It is not enough to confess to God; you must also confess to man, supposing that you have sinned against him. Leave your gift at the altar and go to be reconciled to thy brother. If you have done him a wrong, go and tell him so. If you have defrauded him, whether he knows or not, send him the amount you have taken or kept back, and add to it something to compensate him for his loss. Under the Levitical law it was enacted that the delinquent should restore that which he took violently away, or that about which he had dealt falsely, and should add one fifth part thereto, and only then might he come with his trespass offering to the priest, and be forgiven. This principle holds good to-day. You never will be happy till you have made restitution. Write the letter or make the call at once. And if the one whom you defrauded is no longer alive, then make the debt right with his heirs and representatives. You must roll away this stone from the grave, or the dead joy can never arise, however loudly you may call it to come forth. I do not believe in a repentance which is not noble enough to make amends for the past, so far as they may lie within its reach.

6.—*Give your whole heart once and forever to God.* You may have done it before, but do it again. You may never have done it, then do it for the first time. Kneel down and give yourself, your life, your interests, your all to God. Lay the sacrifice on the altar. If you cannot *give,* then ask God to come, and *take*. Tell Him that you wish to be only, always, all for Him. We might well hesitate to give the Glorious Lord such a handful of withered leaves, if He had not expressly asked us each to give Him our heart. It is very wonderful; but He would not make such a request if He did not really mean it. No doubt He can make something out of our poor nature. A Vessel for His Use. A Weapon for His Hand. A Receptacle for His Glory. A Crown for His Brow.

7.—*Trust God to keep you in all the Future.* The old version used to tell us that He was able to keep us from *falling.* The new version, giving a closer rendering of the Greek, tells us that He is able to guard us from *stumbling.* So He can. So He will. But we must trust Him. Moment by moment we must look into His face, and say, "Hold Thou mine up, and I shall be safe; keep me as the apple of Thine eye; hide me under the shadow of Thy wings." He will never fail thee. He will never fail thee nor forsake thee. He will give His angels charge to keep thee in all thy ways. He will cover thee with His feathers, and under His wing thou shalt trust.

But you say, I fail to look at the moment of temptation. Then do this. Ask the Holy Spirit, whose office it is to bring all things to our remembrance, that He would remind you to look off to Jesus, when you are in danger. Intrust yourself each morning into His hands. Look to Him to keep you looking. Trust in Him to keep you trusting. Do not look at your difficulties or weaknesses. Do not keep thinking that you will some day fall again. Go through life, whispering, saying, singing, a thousand times a day, *Jesus saves me now.*

A friend once told me, that she had been kept from backsliding thus:—She always took time at night to consider quietly in the presence of God, where she had lost ground during the day, and if she felt that she had done so, she never slept until she had asked to be forgiven and restored. 'Tis a good expedient for you and me. Let us repair the little rift within the lute, lest by-and-by it spread and make our music mute, and slowly widening, silence all.

If these directions are followed, the lost chord will be no longer lost, nor shall we have to wait until God's great Angel sounds it, but it will ring again in our heart, and make sweet music in our life.

THE BEST KIND OF LIVING COMES THROUGH DYING

"I am crucified with Christ; nevertheless I live; yet not I, but Christ liveth in me, and the life which I now live in the flesh I live by the faith of the Son of God, who loved me, and gave himself for me."

GALATIANS 2:20

"The supreme fact of history"

WE LOVE TO CLIMB the long, steep hill of Nazareth, to notice our Lord as a child playing with the Syrian boys and girls in the streets; or coming home in the afternoon, grave and demure, from His lessons, received of the old rabbi in the synagogue; or carrying home a piece of carpentry for Joseph. We love also to frequent the Mount of Beatitudes, and listen as He sits and speaks of the lilies, and points to the homeward flight of the birds; and we try to understand the principles that He lays down for His Father's Kingdom. We take pleasure in accompanying Him through the sunny land of Galilee—before Him the crowds of sick, behind Him the throng of the healed—while boys and girls gather round Him, or play in the market-place, calling to their fellows, at perfect ease when He is there, and sure of a kindly look from Him. But after all, neither Nazareth, the Mount of Beatitudes, nor the blessed ministry of Galilee can ever furnish our souls with what they need for the stern battle and ordeal which all of us have to encounter. There is not blood enough in all that; not power and energy enough for doing and suffering: and, therefore, upon certain occasions, we have to make for Calvary, with its tears of blood, and to stand within view of that cross upon which the Redeemer died. It will do us all good to withdraw ourselves, and center our thought upon that supreme fact of history, and our union with it in this far-away vista of the centuries, that we may discover the key note of a perfectly renovated life, as we say, "I have been crucified with Christ: yet I live; and yet no longer I, but Christ liveth in me; and that life which I now live in the flesh I live in faith, the faith which is in the Son of God, who loved me, and gave Himself for me."

Three words form the key notes of this text, namely, the words love, likeness, and life.

"He loved me, and gave Himself for me." When one whom we have known, and who has been well known by the masses of our fellow-countrymen, has suddenly attained to great eminence, and receives a reward either in the conferring of an honorary degree, or the freedom of a city, or in some splendid, magnificent ovation, and when he stands before the admiring crowds, what different degrees there are of interest in his appearance and bearing. There is first the great outside crowd, represented by the man in the street, or the newspaper article writer—these men look upon him as being a great fellow-countryman who has deserved well of his fellows, and they are glad to see his merits appreciated and rewarded. They may forget it all to-morrow, or refer to it as a nine days' wonder. The interest they take is a superficial one compared to that of a more personal nature. There is an inner circle, composed of those who have had some personal relationship with this man. He has been their teacher—in early days they sat at his feet and let his words mould their thought; or he has been a great soldier, and they have followed him, depending on his guidance and generalship in many a hard fight; or as a great statesman he has led his party through defeat and failure to victory. There is a personal element by which some in that crowd are united to him. But even their relationship is not the innermost; for there is another circle represented by his sister, who, as she sees him standing there, remembers how he used to lift her over the stile, and guide her tiny feet across the stepping-stones of the brook; how they played together as boy and girl, roamed the woods for nuts and blackberries in the autumn, or for hyacinths in the spring; and she is glad to see her brother recognized—she almost feels as if she herself were included in his success. But the innermost of all is his wife, who feels that he who stands there belongs to her as he belongs to no man or woman else.

You remember the story of Tygranes, a prince or petty king in Armenia, whose land was conquered by Cyrus. He and his wife were conducted into the presence of the conqueror, and the sentence of death was pronounced according to the barbarous custom of the time. Tygranes, however, pleaded with Cyrus that if necessary he might be exposed to double suffering and torture, in addition to his death, if only his wife might be spared and set free; and Cyrus was so pleased with the man's sincerity and earnestness, that he pardoned them both. When outside the royal pavilion, Tygranes asked his wife what she thought of Cyrus, and she replied: "Indeed, I have no thought for him at all; I thought only of the man who said he was prepared to bear the torture and agony of death for me."

Suppose after that Tygranes had been suddenly elevated to a front place in the world, and that all men had done him honor; don't you think she would have prided herself on a tie between him and her which no one else could emulate? Would she not say: "That man whom they admire loves me, and gave, or offered to give, himself for me."

There is no man or woman who may not look on Jesus

Christ in that way. We know that He is exalted to the right hand of power; the universe is a unit because He is the center of it, and concentric circles of all moral and spiritual beings circle around Him as He stands in the midst of the throne; but amid all the myriads that turn to Him, there is no one who may not feel that there is a tie, an affinity between Jesus Christ and him or her, which enables us to affirm, as though there were no other being in all the universe: "He loved *me*, and gave Himself for *me*. I am His bride, His body, His other self."

On a moonlit night there may be a million people standing on the margin of a great sea, all looking in the same direction, but for each there is a moonlit path across the water. In the same way—though at this moment I am one of the millions of souls standing before the Lamb who may participate in His redeeming love—the pathway of His glorious light comes to my feet, and makes to sparkle the wavelets that break upon the shore. I want you to say that. You shrink, and say it is too much for such as you. Yet, notwithstanding your protestations, you are perfectly justified in making that allegation (1) because it rests upon the universal testimony of this Book. We are told: "He is the propitiation for the sins of the whole world," and inasmuch as you are one of "the world," He must have made the propitiation for *your* sin. We are told: "He died for all"; therefore, again, He must have died for you. We are told that His blood was shed for the remission of sins of all those who are included in the moral lapse which has overtaken our race; and if you have been overcome by sin, and if there are premonitory symptoms of death in your body, it proves that you have a perfect right to claim that redemption which is as wide as the family of man. (2) It rests upon the nature of the

100

case. We are told that it was "by the Eternal Spirit" that Jesus offered Himself to God. Now the essence of the eternal is this—that the eternal is present at any one point or moment of time, as though there were no other moment. Therefore the whole weight of the eternal is present in your life, and you have as much right to put in your claim for the whole benefit of the death of Christ as though no one else in the whole universe shared it. (3) You have a perfect right to make that allegation, because if you exclude yourself, everyone might, and that would neutralize the whole work of Christ. The fact is that everyone feels just as you—equally unfit to utter these words.

When someone asked Dr. Parker, "Why did Christ choose Judas?" he replied, "I cannot tell; but I know a greater mystery—Why did He choose *me?*" Everyone cries, "Oh, it is wonderful that I have been chosen!" Even Calvin, the great theologian, when he comes to write about this, lays his pen down, and gives up his commentating, and says it is difficult to find words to express the wonder of it. There he leaves it. The experience of your heart is only that which every holy soul has had, and yet they dared to affirm it, as you may.

Do you not also feel a pull at your heart that you would like it to be true? Do you not, in your secret soul, say: "If only an angel were to flash from the heavens and whisper in my ear that Jesus thought of me on the cross, and made atonement for my sin, I would hardly be able to sleep for very joy"? If you feel like that, it is a love-token from Christ. The Spirit of God has put it in your heart, and He would not have done so if were not true. "No man knoweth the things of a man save the spirit of a man that is in him," and if the Spirit of Christ has put into your heart the secret yearning for the love of God, does not that prove there is an affinity between your heart and His? If it were not so He would have told you. He would never have led you to this point. And inasmuch as the leaping of the magnet to the steel-filing, or the needle to the magnet, proves the affinity between them, so the leaping of your heart towards Jesus Christ to-day proves your affinity with Him, and enables you to say, however unworthy you are: "He loved me, and gave Himself for me." So that you may single out our Lord to-day, amid all the crowd of the blessed ones, and pick Him out for yourself, and feel as Tygranes' wife felt towards Tygranes. You may say, "I am needed by Christ, required by Him; His heaven will not be complete without me; that He might have me with Him for ever. He loved me, and gave Himself for me." Charles Kingsley wished that there should be inscribed upon the tombstone of his wife and himself, these words:

Amavimus, amamus, amabimus.
(We loved, we love, we shall love.)

And you and I may say the same, "Amavit, amat, amabit"—
"He loved, He loves, He will love."

Professor Elmslie said that no one would ever be able to deny that he had preached the love of Christ. When he lay dying, he said to his wife, "Kate, God is Love—is all Love; we must live to tell the people so, especially our boy. You must do that. We must tell the people that God is Love." And if I were you, I would say—not because you understand it, or feel it, for in one sense it does seem a terrible mistake on Christ's part to have come to woo such fickle hearts as ours—but say over and over again, until you realize the truth of it: "He loved me,

102

and gave Himself for me. If a millionaire gives himself for
a pauper, if a parent gives himself for his child, if the
just gives himself for the unjust, though it seems a poor
bargain, there is nothing more to say about it; but, oh,
the bliss of it!

You cannot come to my second division until you
apprehend the first; and you can only know the first by
voluntary will, choice and purpose. But the next step is
that the fundamental principles upon which Jesus acted,
and which were involved in His Cross, should become
the fundamental principles of your life, which henceforth shall be lived, not to self, but to Him. What were
the principles upon which Christ lived, and that brought
Him ultimately to Calvary?

1.—His unity with the will of God. That word
atonement has been greatly mispronounced. Let us agree
to call it *at-one-ment*. When our Lord came to the world
He announced as His program that He had come to do
the will of God; and from the first to the last He was at
one with the will of God, as a harmonium and piano, or
an organ and cornet may be in accord. Do you remember
the four occasions when He chose God's will? First, at
the waters of baptism, when He passed under the lintel
of God's will, and said: "It becometh us (Me and you) to
do My Father's will." Next, on the plateau of the desert, where He stood face to face with the temptation to
have an easier life, when for one act of wrong He was to
secure the government of the world; "No, away with it,"
He said; "I am going to take the Father's plan, though it
means suffering, and finally, death. I am going to *win* the
crown." And again, on the Mount of Transfiguration—
which I always think was the turning-point of His
life—six months before He died, He turned His back

upon the open door to paradise, and said: "I will not spare Myself, but will take the path lined with cypresses, that ends in the cross, because it is My Father's will." And then in the Garden of Gethsemane, as you all know, when the bloody sweat stood on His brow and dropped thence to the ground, He said: "I will drink the cup My Father gives Me, since it is His will."

If you and I want to follow in His dear steps through the world, we must let the will of God be our master, and we must build our lives according to the pattern shown us in the Mount. We must apply the will of God as a test to the details of daily life. We must acquire that habit of not even planning a summer holiday, until we are absolutely certain that the plan of God lies that way. I don't believe that Jesus was ever insensible to the will of God. He never saw a bird fall to the ground but He knew that somehow it was included in the will of God; He never saw a flower crushed under foot but He knew that somehow that was included in the will of God. And when we have learned to love and consult the will of God, when everything in life is determined by that law of gravitation—not only the great planets of our life, but the molecules of dust driven by the wind—then we are on the track of Christ. The will of God always means death to the self life; but from the ground there shall blossom red, joy that shall endless be. It takes long years of mistakes and failures, grazed elbows and broken knees, before at last we are broken in and harnessed to the will of God. But in doing that will, there is great reward.

2.—The second great thought of our Lord was not only to be at one with the Father's will, but to be dead to the world which cast Him out—dead to it in so far as its applause or frown, its methods or principles might be considered.

The Best Kind of Living Comes Through Dying

Mr. Jowett tells us of a man in his congregation who was dead to his past. I think he rose in the church-meeting and said: "For forty years I have lived in the service of the world, and have done its behests; and I am sorry for it. But when I stand before the Father, God, if any of those days should rise in judgment and condemn me, I will say: The man you describe is dead, and buried, and done for, and I refuse to answer to his name, or bear the charges made against his life." If I am speaking to anyone who is carrying a heavy millstone round his neck because haunted by an old and sinful past, which he feels will dog his steps through life, remember that the Cross of Jesus is an absolute break with the past.

Then there is a deadness to the pleasures of the world. I remember a lady in New York, with whom I had the honor to be acquainted, who, coming back one night from the ball where she had been the leader of the dance, threw aside her ball-dress, and said: "Farewell, O heartless and proud world! I have done with thee for ever; and from now I devote myself to Jesus Christ." When I met her again, three or four years ago, I found she had been the means of saving 800 fallen girls off the streets.

This deadness means deadness to death. Those who have died once in Jesus have died to death. There is no second death; they do not taste of death. I believe death to us who are really crucified is only like a signal man in the railway box, who has been manipulating the red, white and blue lights, for whom the hour strikes when he should go off duty; and as he trudges through the mist and slush to his home, he sees the lights burning for him from the window, he knows the kettle is singing on the hob, that wife and child will greet him. And at last he takes off his heavy, soaked coat at the door, and goes in to sit with them. So we shall just take off the coat of this body, and go in to sit down with our Beloved—that is what people call death. We, however, need have no fear or care for it.

3.—Remember, also, that Jesus Christ was animated by an unconquerable love for men. He was held to that cross, not by Pilate or Caiaphas, not by the nails driven into His hands and feet, but by an unconquerable passion for us—for you, and me, and for all. It was the love of Christ that constrained Him, bound Him, transfixed Him, and held Him. I do not know how it is with you, but I am so far from it, I hardly dare to preach about it. I have lived all these years, and I know, looking back, that there has been a sense of duty in my ministry, and too little of that unconquerable passion which brought Jesus Christ to die! I think I could kneel with reverence before the man or woman who was animated by an unconquerable passion for this lost world; but they are rare to find. Many of us have been so callous; we have sat down and watched the crucifixion of mankind; have looked unmoved upon the torture to which many have been exposed. In the papers I read the story of a man brought before the police court for cruelty to his wife and children. He would eat all the victuals that the poor woman had earned and prepared for her starving children, while they stood watching him; but he would give them neither bite nor crumb. That man was sentenced to six months, and deserved all he got. Yet we must not be too quick to judge; for how often we have eaten the Bread of the Living Christ, whilst the world was starving for hunger? We have so little of that glow of holy passion for souls. How difficult it is to understand!

Brainard tells us in his journal that one day when the trees were bare of leaves, and an icy wind breathed through the forest, to use his own words, "from when the sun was held an hour high till the stars appeared," he was wrestling for his poor Indians, until the sweat stood upon his skin, in spite of the chilly air. Are there any amongst us here who would do that sort of thing— who would wrestle the livelong day until, in a frosty air, the sweat stood upon them? We seem to be only little children, wading in the shallows; yet, if we were to take the steps I have indicated so far, if we were constrained by the Love of Christ, appropriated the Life of Christ for ourselves, and lived in God's will as He did, there would also be given to us to travail, as the apostle did, in birth for the souls of men. Who was this man? He was "less than the least of all saints." One of the old Puritans said: "I do not find fault with Paul for saying what he did; but for pushing me out of my place." "Less than the least of all saints." None of us can have that place—long since it has been taken by Paul; and if he was "less than the least," and yet was loved by the Son of God, there is no one here who is not included in the scope of these words. Only don't exclude yourselves.

There is the word *Live*. As soon as *you* say "No" to "I," *Christ* says "I." You say "No" to self, and "Yes" to Christ. Like the revolving doors in the big hotels of London which, as they emit one man, admit another. If you pass yourself out, you pass Christ in by the same act of revolution.

I refuse to water it down and say the *influence* of Christ, when the apostle says, "Christ liveth in me." We protest against that word *influence* being inserted here, unless it is taken as meaning that the life of Jesus literally flows into the soul. Look at the mantle of the gaslight so often in use, and see how it glows with light. Think of the electric spark that lives in the carbon. Similarly the life of Christ Himself should become our source of radiance and power. We see God in the glow-worm's torch, in the dewdrop, in the song of the bird, in the flash and roll of planet and sun, and we cannot think that He stands outside of us as only an influence. No; believe that it is literally true, that Jesus Christ does come to live in the spirit that is open to Him. When Paul said, "I live by the faith of the Son of God," he probably means faith *in* the Son of God; but it may also mean the faith of the open heart of Jesus towards the Father. To quote His own words: "The Living Father hath sent Me, and I live by the Father; so he that eateth Me shall live by Me." In sanctification a time arrives when the door of partition between Christ and our spirit is so broken down that He comes to and fro without reserve, entreaty, or introduction, and the very life of the Son of God wells up in thought and speech, in smile and tear-brimming eye. I believe that a real Incarnation of Christ may be your experience and mine.

"The life that I now live in the flesh"—still in the flesh—with father, mother, sister, child, friend. It is a natural life, nothing strained or unreal; just the life that ordinary people live in the flesh; but we are called to live it with our hearts open towards our Lord, so that as our Head and Life, He may work in us to will and to do of His own good pleasure.

> 'Tis life of which our veins are scant;
> 'Tis life, O life, for which we pant.

Does anyone say, "This is impossible"? I want you to remember how impossible it must have seemed to Saul of Tarsus, when he was rejecting Christ, and persecuting those who belonged to Christ, that ever he could use words like these. Surely what was true for him may be true for the most unlikely person here. "O taste and see that the Lord is good."

THE OUTLOOK, BACKLOOK AND UPLOOK

"Behold, I see the heavens, opened, and the Son of man standing on the right hand of God."

ACTS 7:56

THE PRIMITIVE CHURCH was approaching a very critical moment in its story. Six years must have elapsed since our Lord bade His disciples go into all the world and preach the Gospel to every creature; but they were still tarrying in Jerusalem. There is a significant sentence in one of the previous chapters which says: "The number of the disciples were multiplied in Jerusalem greatly," and the emphasis upon that word Jerusalem indicates that the Church was on the eve of a forward movement when Jerusalem would cease to be the home and focus of the Church, which would be sent forth to the uttermost parts of the earth.

It is rather remarkable, however, that this forward movement did not begin with the beckoning hand of the Son of God, or with any voice or vision, but with a very tiny thread of circumstance, and, indeed, it is on these trivial events that some of the greatest movements of history impinge.

The Jews in Jerusalem were composed of two great branches, the Hebrews of the Hebrews, and the Jews which had been brought up in Alexandria and in other Greek-speaking lands, but who had returned to Jerusalem to settle there in business or to die. Great numbers of each of these two classes had been drawn into the Church. As we know, the poorer members in that Church lived upon the gifts of the richer, of men like Barnabas, who had sold their land and shared out their property. There had been some considerable murmuring and irrita-

113

tion, especially among the poor widows belonging to the Hellenist branch, with respect to the insufficiency and irregularity of the doles given to them, and out of that ferment between a number of poor widows came this great forward movement of the Church.

Peter had no idea what he was really advancing when he spoke about the choice of these deacons; but they were to provide the forward movement of the Church, which from that moment passed largely out of the hands of the apostles into the hands of this wonderful foreign element. The apostles up to this minute, for six years, had not only given themselves up to spiritual, but to secular work; but they now felt that the time had come when there must be a division between these two offices, and while they gave themselves to the spiritual, others should be called in to relieve them of the service of tables. But you will notice how careful they were to affirm that whatever was done in connection with the Church, though it should be the distribution of alms, should be done by spiritual men—"Choose ye out men, full of the Holy Ghost and of wisdom, whom we may appoint over this business." It is also interesting to notice that the whole multitude, guided by the Divine Spirit, selected the deacons, and they were afterwards brought to the apostles to be set apart by the laying on of hands, and by prayer.

The leader of these seven deacons was Stephen. His name was curiously prophetic. It means "the man who was crowned." Stephen, in any case, was a well-tried man, who had perhaps known the Son of man after the flesh, and who at this moment was called to lead the forward movement of the Church. A sunny nature, sincere, pure, beautiful, strong and wise. This young man, a Hellenist, stood forth in the early Church as the pioneer of the greatest movement of history. It is of him we are told that within sight of death, a cruel death, he looked up and saw heaven opened, and the Son of man, not sitting, as they had been accustomed to suppose, but standing as though eager to see his fate, to succour, and to welcome him.

We are told that they looked upon his face and saw that it had an angel look. His soul looked out at that moment, and because it was a rare, pure, generous, and beautiful soul, it irradiated the very veil of the flesh through which it looked upon his accusers and foes.

We can only note some few words employed to describe Stephen, which indicate how holy a man he was. There are three sentences. First, the multitude chose Stephen, who was "full of faith and of the Holy Ghost." Faith, of course, you will remember, differs from belief, for belief simply holds as credible some statement made to it, while faith links itself to the timeless, to the invisible, and the eternal. "Full of faith." There was an open passage for shafts of light to pass between heaven and Stephen's soul. He was also "full of the Holy Ghost." It is remarkable that this word is used of him. There are three words used that deserve to be compared. We are told that Peter was suddenly "filled" for special work, but he could be as suddenly emptied; we are told in Acts 13 that the dwellers in the highlands of Galatia were "being filled" all the time, as when a running brook keeps a lake full to the brim; but in the case of Stephen we are told that he was "full," as though his inner life were fed from some unknown spring, which, rising in his soul, was able to keep him from ever dipping down an inch beneath the brim of fulness.

Second, we are told in another brief sentence that he was "full of grace and power." A most exquisite combination. Grace—generosity, sweetness, tenderness, sympathy, which made the widows' hearts leap for joy when his voice was heard in the entry, or his step on the stair. Grace and power. There was something in his presence that lifted people from despair, from disease, from despondency and death, to life; something thrilled through him and vibrated from him. Third, they could not resist the wisdom or power or spirit with which he spoke. Such was Stephen, God's rare gift to the early Church.

We can easily understand the course of events. As soon as he was elected, he went throughout Jerusalem with his gifts for the poor widows. Wherever he entered, he was like a sunbeam, left a trail of laughter and joy behind him. People cared more for the hand that gave the dole than for the dole itself. It was the way he did it that made everybody love him. As he went to the houses of the poor believers, he came in contact with their children and relatives and friends. When he spoke with them they disputed, and the disputing grew from day to day until it reached the court of the synagogue in which the Hellenists met.

There were three branches of these Greek-speaking Jews—the Libertines, freedmen who had come back from Pompey's wars, or the children of those that had been freed and had come back to settle in Jerusalem; there were also the Hellenist Jews of the African seaboard, of Alexandria and Cyrene; and, thirdly, the Hellenists of Cilicia. In that last word we catch sight of Saul of Tarsus; and thus these two young men came into collision. The great battles of the Church with the world have always been in the hands of young men. Finally, since this great synagogue could not crush Stephen by argument, they suborned witnesses who laid information that he had spoken against Moses and the law. He was at once arrested by order of the court, and dragged away to prison. In a few hours the Sanhedrin met, and he found himself standing face to face with a crowd of infuriated, scowling Hebrews. It was then, as he waited for his turn to speak and the people were looking on him, that his soul dwelling within the temple of his nature was illumined from the Divine Spirit and shone through the veil. The Holy Spirit was in his soul like fire, and poured forth like glowing metal his grace, faith, wisdom, power, and sweetness, all combined in one pure beam of celestial glory; and to those who beheld Stephen's face it was as though it were the face of an angel. Such is the outlook of the saintly soul.

Some of us have read the apology of Socrates before he drank the cup of hemlock, and Newman's *Apologia pro vita sua*, but how incomparably noble is this of Stephen's. He knew the Scriptures, his soul had been nourished by them, and was saturated by them. He not only knew the letter, but had absorbed the spirit. He looked upon the Bible as a statesman, and saw the great underlying principles of God's covenant. You will never understand the Bible if you read it out of a little morning text-book. Stephen had broad views of God's movements. He saw Him move widely through the world, and loved to detect the great principles on which his government was based.

1. Stephen saw the broadening and widening development of God's purpose. He saw that all through the Jewish history there had been movement, never stagnation. He saw that Abram was called alone, and after much journeying was led to settle in Canaan, where very slowly the patriarchal family grew into a nation; he saw how the Israelites went down to Joseph some seventy persons, but it took 400 years before they became a

nation and emerged at the Exodus; he saw how in the wilderness the whole state of the Hebrew civilization lay in a nutshell, which took long centuries to evolve under Solomon and the kings, and it was as though he said to himself, "It is impossible to suppose that the Hebrew race is to stagnate always in Jerusalem; if we follow the history of the past, we must still move and advance."

2. He loved to dwell on the fact that each new stage of movement had been inaugurated by one individual, who at first had been rejected, despised, and perhaps done to death. For instance Abram had to leave his family, Joseph was cast out by his brethren, Moses had to flee to Midian from his own people, and in the wilderness they repeatedly threatened his life. Invariably the great leaders of the Jewish people had been treated with injury, afflicted, exiled, tormented and killed, from which he inferred that it was not surprising that they had killed the Christ. The rejection and crucifixion of the Lord was in a line with the whole Hebrew story of the past.

3. He insisted that the temple of which they made so much, with its priesthood and services, was not necessary to the integrity of the Hebrew race; and with a sure foresight of what was coming when Titus would destroy the city, he said that even though the temple should be levelled to the dust, and the priesthood scattered, and the sacrifices should no longer smoke upon the altar, yet the genius of true religion was independent of these outward symbols, and would express itself in other and loftier forms. This religion did not need tabernacle or temple, but could exist in the hearts of men. These were the three great thoughts that this young Hellenist, so eloquent, so devout, so forcible, deduced

from the comprehensive study of the Old Testament. There you have the broad outlook of the prophet.

At the end of his long apology, he turned to his audience and applied it. This aroused them. People are quite prepared for you to give them an historical compendium, quite prepared for you to recite the story of the great past, but just so soon as you apply the lessons of history and show that the same evil which goaded their forefathers to wrong deeds is still present with the children; that we are always coming back to the sins of those who have preceded us, to their blindness and superstition—directly you say that, you must expect the gnashing of teeth, the swift onslaught upon the witness. When he came to apply the Scripture, they stopped their ears, and ran on him with one accord, and it was at that moment that he said with absolute composure, "I see."

All who surrounded him were as blind as bats in daylight; the only one who was capable of receiving the heavenly vision was this young man whose soul was glowing with celestial heroism and fire. He alone could say, "I see." The curtain was rent, the glory that shone on Sinai was shining within his vision, and he seemed to say, "The Son of man, whom I knew, with whom I lived and walked and talked, I see Him, not sitting indifferent, but standing, alert, regnant, looking down on me from the right hand of God."

And that look might be yours and mine every day. If only we were filled with God's Holy Spirit, we also might have that look into the holy place, for where the Holy Ghost is in the heart, we always see Jesus, we always see the Son of man, we always see Him standing for us. Have you seen Jesus standing there for you?

When Dr. Parker was quite a young lad, he was

accustomed to hold arguments with infidels outside the great iron works on Tyneside. One day an infidel challenged him upon this great passage, and said, "What did God do for Stephen?" insinuating that if there had been a God, He would have interposed to rescue him from the hands of his foes. Dr. Parker always said he believed that it was given to him in the same hour what he should say, and he answered, "What did God do for him? He gave him the power to pray for the forgiveness of those who stoned him." It was a great answer.

What did that look do? It did three things. First, it enabled him to commit his spirit to Christ. You might have thought that when he felt his poor body being battered, he would have said, "If God cannot take care of my body, He cannot of my spirit," but that look to the risen Christ enabled him to say, although his body was being shamefully disfigured, "This is all that they can do; now I commend myself to Thee; Lord Jesus, receive my spirit." Second, he was able to forgive, "Lay not this sin to their charge." Third, he was able, mid the crashing stones, so we are told, "to fall asleep." Fall asleep! that is what you and I did last night, tired out. Fall asleep! that is what the babe does at your breast. Fall asleep! that is what the weary pilgrim does in his downy bed, with his wife and child at his side. But that Stephen should fall asleep outside the city, amid the crashing stones, that was the result of the upward look. And one young man never forgot it. Stephen's dying look was one of the goads against the pricks of which Saul kicked in vain. He could not explain it, could not contradict it, could not get over it; but in his quiet hours at night, or when travelling alone, the face of that dying man came back with that supernatural glow upon it, and it led him finally to take Stephen's place, and to be stoned

"Lay not this sin to their charge"

as Stephen was. Such is the uplook of the martyr.

Stephen first led the martyred host, first carried his cross after Christ, first meekly trod the way of pain, first crossed the bridge, and as Augustine said, "he left the bridge behind him." May we follow in his train because we have received that same indwelling Spirit, who waits to fill our hearts also with the martyr's spirit.

THE SECRET OF GUIDANCE

*"I will instruct thee and teach thee in the way which thou shalt go
I will guide thee with mine eye."*

PSALM 32:8

MANY CHILDREN OF GOD are so deeply exercised on the matter of guidance that it may be helpful to give a few suggestions as to knowing the way in which our Father would have us walk, and the work he would have us do. The importance of the subject cannot be exaggerated; so much of our power and peace consists in knowing where God would have us be, and in being just there.

The manna only falls where the cloudy pillar broods; but it is certain to be found on the sands, which a few hours ago were glistening in the flashing light of the heavenly fire, and are now shadowed by the fleecy canopy of cloud. If we are precisely where our heavenly Father would have us to be, we are perfectly sure that He will provide food and raiment, and everything beside. When He sends His servants to Cherith, He will make even the ravens to bring them food.

How much of our Christian work has been abortive, because we have persisted in initiating it for ourselves, instead of ascertaining what God was doing, and where He required our presence. We dream bright dreams of success. We try and command it. We call to our aid all kinds of expedients, questionable or otherwise. And at last we turn back, disheartened and ashamed, like children who are torn and scratched by the brambles, and soiled by the quagmire. None of this had come about, if only we had been, from the first, under God's unerring guidance. He might test us, but he could not allow us to mistake.

Naturally, the child of God, longing to know his Father's will, turns to the sacred Book, and refreshes his confidence by noticing how in all ages God has guided those who dared to trust Him up to the very hilt, but who, at the time, must have been as perplexed as we are often now. We know how Abraham left kindred and country, and started, with no other guide than God, across the trackless desert to a land which he knew not. We know how for forty years the Israelites were led through the peninsula of Sinai, with its labyrinths of red sand-stone and its wastes of sand. We know how Joshua, in entering the Land of Promise, was able to cope with the difficulties of an unknown region, and to overcome great and warlike nations, because he looked to the Captain of the Lord's host, who ever leads to victory. We know how, in the early Church, the Apostles were enabled to thread their way through the most difficult questions, and to solve the most perplexing problems; laying down principles which will guide the Church to the end of time; and this because it was revealed to them as to what they should do and say, by the Holy Spirit.

The promises for guidance are unmistakable, Psalm 32:8: "I will instruct thee and teach thee in the way which thou shalt go." This is God's distinct assurance to those whose transgressions are forgiven, and whose sins are covered, and who are more quick to notice the least symptom of His will, than horse or mule to feel the bit.

Prov. 7:6: "In all thy ways acknowledge Him, and He shall direct (or make plain) thy paths." A sure word, on which we may rest; if only we fulfil the previous conditions, of trusting with all our heart, and of not leaning to our own understanding.

Isa. 58:11: "The Lord shall guide thee continually." It is impossible to think that He could guide us at all, if He

126

did not guide us always. For the greatest events of life, like the huge rocking-stones in the west of England, revolve on the smallest points. A pebble may alter the flow of a stream. The growth of a grain of mustard seed may determine the rainfall of a continent. Thus we are bidden to look for a Guidance which shall embrace the whole of life in all its myriad necessities.

John 8:12: "I am the light of the world; he that followeth Me shall not walk in darkness, but shall have the light of life." The reference here seems to be to the wilderness wanderings; and the Master promises to be to all faithful souls, in their pilgrimage to the City of God, what the cloudy pillar was to the children of Israel on their march to the Land of Promise.

These are but specimens. The vault of Scripture is inlaid with thousands such, that glisten in their measure as the stars which guide the wanderer across the deep. Well may the prophet sum up the heritage of the servants of the Lord by saying of the Holy City, "All thy children shall be taught of the Lord, and great shall be the peace of thy children."

And yet it may appear to some tried and timid hearts as if every one mentioned in the Word of God was helped, but they are left without help. They seem to have stood before perplexing problems, face to face with life's mysteries, eagerly longing to know what to do, but no angel has come to tell them, and no iron gate has opened to them in the prison-house of circumstances.

Some lay the blame on their own stupidity. Their minds are blunt and dull. They cannot catch God's meaning, which would be clear to others. They are so nervous of doing wrong, that they cannot learn clearly what is right. "Who is blind, but my servant? or deaf, as my messenger that I sent? Who is blind as he that is perfect, and blind as the Lord's servant?" Yet, how do we treat our children? One child is so bright-witted and so keen that a little hint is enough to indicate the way; another was born dull: it cannot take in your meaning quickly. Do you only let the clever one know what you want? Will you not take the other upon your knee and make clear to it the directions which baffle it? Does not the distress of the tiny nursling, who longs to know that it may immediately obey, weave an almost stronger bond than that which binds you to the rest? Oh! weary, perplexed, and stupid children, believe in the great love of God, and cast yourselves upon it, sure that he will come down to your ignorance, and suit Himself to your needs, and will take "the lambs in His arms, and carry them in His bosom, and *gently lead* those that are with young."

There are certain practical directions which we must attend to in order that we may be led into the mind of the Lord.

1.—*Our Motives must be Pure.* "When thine eye is single, thy whole body is also full of light" (Luke 11:34). You have been much in darkness lately, and perhaps this passage will point the reason. Your eye has not been single. There has been some obliquity of vision. A spiritual squint. And this has hindered you from discerning indications of God's will, which otherwise had been as clear as noonday.

We must be very careful in judging our motives: searching them as the detectives at the doors of the House of Commons search each stranger who enters. When, by the grace of God, we have been delivered from grosser forms of sin, we are still liable to the subtle working of self in our holiest and loveliest hours. It poisons our motives. It breathes decay on our fairest fruit-bearing. It whispers seductive flatteries into our pleased ears. It turns the spirit from its holy purpose as the masses of iron on ocean steamers deflect the needle of the compass from the pole.

So long as there is some thought of personal advantage, some idea of acquiring the praise and commendation of men, some aim at self-aggrandizement, it will be simply impossible to find out God's purpose concerning us. The door must be resolutely shut against all this, if we would hear the still small voice. All cross-lights must be excluded, if we would see the Urim and Thummim stone brighten with God's "Yes," or darken with his "No."

Ask the Holy Spirit to give you the single eye, and to inspire in your heart one aim alone; that which animated our Lord, and enabled Him to cry, as He reviewed His life, "I have glorified Thee on earth." Let this be the watchword of our lives, "Glory to God in the highest." Then our "whole body shall be full of light, having no part dark, as when the bright shining of a candle doth give light."

2.—*Our Will must be Surrendered.* "My judgment is just; because I seek not Mine own will, but the will of the Father which hath sent Me" (John 5:30). This was the secret, which Jesus not only practiced, but taught. In one form or another He was constantly insisting on a surrendered will, as the key to perfect knowledge, "If any man will do His will, he shall know."

There is all the difference between a will which is extinguished and one which is surrendered. God does not demand that our wills should be crushed out, like the sinews of a fakir's unused arm. He only asks that they should say "Yes" to Him. Pliant to Him as the willow twig to the practiced hand.

Many a time, as the steamer has neared the quay, have

I watched the little lad take his place beneath the poop, with eye and ear fixed on the captain, and waiting to shout each word he utters to the grimy engineers below; and often have I longed that my will should repeat as accurately, and as promptly, the words and will of God, that all the lower nature might obey.

It is for the lack of this subordination that we so often miss the guidance we seek. There is a secret controversy between our will and God's. And we shall never be right till we have let Him take, and break, and make. Oh! do seek for that. If you cannot give, let Him take. If you are not willing, confess that you are willing to be made willing. Hand yourself over to Him to work in you, to will and to do of His own good pleasure. We must be as plastic clay, ready to take any shape that the great Potter may choose, so shall we be able to detect His guidance.

3.—*We must seek Information for our Mind.* This is certainly the next step. God has given us these wonderful faculties of brain power, and He will not ignore them. In grace He does not cancel the action of any of His marvelous bestowments, but He uses them for the communication of His purposes and thoughts.

It is of the greatest importance, then, that we should feed our minds with facts; with reliable information; with the results of human experience, and above all, with the teachings of the Word of God. It is matter for the utmost admiration to notice how full the Bible is of biography and history: so that there is hardly a single crisis in our lives that may not be matched from those wondrous pages. There is no book like the Bible for casting a light on the dark landings of human life.

We have no need or right to run hither and thither to ask our friends what we ought to do; but there is no harm in our taking pains to gather all reliable information, on which the flame of holy thought and consecrated purpose may feed and grow strong. It is for us ultimately to decide as God shall teach us, but His voice may come to us through the voice of sanctified commonsense, acting on the materials we have collected. Of course at times God may bid us act against our reason; but these are very exceptional; and then our duty will be so clear that there can be no mistake. But for the most part God will speak in the results of deliberate consideration, weighing and balancing the *pros* and *cons*.

When Peter was shut up in prison, and could not possibly extricate himself, an angel was sent to do for him what he could not do for himself; but when they had passed through a street or two of the city, the angel left him to consider the matter for himself. Thus God treats us still. He will dictate a miraculous course by miraculous methods. But when the ordinary light of reason is adequate to the task, He will leave us to act as occasion may serve.

4.—*We must be much in Prayer for Guidance.* The Psalms are full of earnest pleadings for clear direction: "Show me Thy way, O Lord, lead me in a plain path, because of mine enemies." It is the law of our Father's house that His children shall ask for what they want. "If any man lack wisdom, let him ask of God, who giveth all men liberally, and upbraideth not."

In a time of change and crisis, we need to be much in prayer, not only on our knees, but in that sweet form of inward prayer, in which the spirit is constantly offering itself up to God, asking to be shown His will; soliciting that it may be impressed upon its surface, as the heavenly bodies photograph themselves on prepared paper. Wrapt in prayer like this the truthful believer may tread the deck of the ocean steamer night after night, sure that He who points the stars their courses will not fail to direct the soul which has no other aim than to do His will.

One good form of prayer at such a juncture is to ask that doors may be shut, that the way may be closed, and that all enterprises which are not according to God's will may be arrested at their very beginning. Put the matter absolutely into God's hands from the outset, and He will not fail to shatter the project and defeat the aim which is not according to His holy will.

5.—*We must wait the gradual unfolding of God's plan in Providence.* God's impressions within and His word without are always corroborated by His Providence around, and we should quietly wait until these three focus into one point.

Sometimes it looks as if we are bound to act. Every one says we must do something; and indeed things seem to have reached so desperate a pitch that we must. Behind are the Egyptians; right and left are inaccessible precipices; before is the sea. It is not easy at such times to stand still and see the salvation of God; but we must. When Saul compelled himself, and offered sacrifice, because he thought that Samuel was too late in coming, he made the great mistake of his life.

God may delay to come in the guise of His Providence. There was delay ere Sennacherib's host lay like withered leaves around the Holy City. There was delay ere Jesus came walking on the sea in the early dawn, or hastened to raise Lazarus. There was delay ere the angel sped to Peter's side on the night before his expected martyrdom. He stays long enough to test patience of faith, but not a moment behind the extreme hour of need. "The vision is yet for an appointed time, but at the end it shall speak, and shall not lie; though it tarry, wait for it; because it will surely come; it will not tarry."

It is very remarkable how God guides us by circumstances. At one moment the way may seem utterly blocked, and then shortly afterwards some trivial incident occurs, which might not seem much to others, but which to the keen eye of faith speaks volumes. Sometimes these signs are repeated in different ways in answer to prayer. They are not haphazard results of chance, but the opening up of circumstances in the direction in which we should walk. And they begin to multiply, as we advance towards our goal, just as lights do as we near a populous town, when darting through the land by night express.

Sometimes men sigh for an angel to come to point them their way: that simply indicates that as yet the time has not come for them to move. If you do not know what you ought to do, stand still until you do. And when the time comes for action, circumstances, like glow-worms, will sparkle along your path; and you will become so sure that you are right, when God's three witnesses concur, that you could not be surer though an angel beckoned you on.

The circumstances of our daily life are to us an infallible indication of God's will, when they concur with the inward promptings of the Spirit and with the Word of God. So long as they are stationary, wait. When you must act, they will open, and a way will be made through oceans and rivers, wastes and rocks.

We often make a great mistake, thinking that God is not guiding us at all, because we cannot see far in front. But this is not His method. He only undertakes that *the steps* of a good man should be ordered by the Lord. Not next year, but to-morrow. Not the next mile, but the next yard. Not the whole pattern, but the next stitch in the canvas. If you expect more than this you will be disappointed, and get back into the dark. But this will secure for you leading in the right way, as you will acknowledge when you review it from the hill-tops of glory.

We cannot ponder too deeply the lessons of the cloud given in the exquisite picture-lesson on Guidance (Num. 9:15-23). Let us look high enough for guidance. Let us encourage our soul to wait only upon God till it is given. Let us cultivate that meekness which He will guide in judgment. Let us seek to be of quick understanding, that we may be apt to see the least sign of His will. Let us stand with girded loins and lighted lamps, that we may be prompt to obey. Blessed are those servants. They shall be led by a right way to the golden city of the saints.

Speaking for myself, after months of waiting and prayer, I have become absolutely sure of the Guidance of my heavenly Father; and with the emphasis of personal experience, I would encourage each troubled and perplexed soul that may read these lines to wait patiently for the Lord, until He clearly indicates His will.

A KINGDOM FOR YOU

"Ye are they which have continued with me in my temptations. And i appoint unto you a kingdom, as my Father hath appointed unto me."

LUKE 22:28, 29

LORD TENNYSON described King Arthur and the companions of his Round Table. I have to speak to you about a greater King and His companions as they gathered round the table for the last Supper. But there were not many traces of royalty about the King. The popularity which three years before had greeted Him had long since ebbed away, and many that had been profuse in their protestations of devotion had thought discretion the better part of valour, and were notably absentees. A handful only of peasants and fishermen, not specially distinguished from those who were plying their craft in and round the Lake of Galilee, were gathered around that table; the meshes of His foes were being drawn ever closer around Him, and were destined within a few hours to drag Him to His doom.

Jesus Christ, as He sat there, was not at all a King according to any earthly model, or the expectations of His people; He knew, indeed, most certainly what was awaiting Him within the next few hours. He said, "With desire I have desired to eat this Passover with you before I suffer." He evidently expected that that pascal lamb was to provide Him sustenance and comfort amid the terrible ordeal He anticipated. As that lamb had been roast with fire, so was He to pass through the fever of the cross. Those bitter herbs, and all the accompaniments of that simple feast, told Him the same story. Indeed, He knew that the very man was present who would betray

Him, and that Judas would certainly within a very few hours perform the fatal deed.

He knew that He was going along the predestined path; for He said Himself, "The Son of Man goeth as it was determined." The path which had been predetermined before the world was made, which had been prefigured by every Passover which had returned year after year, which had inspired some of the loftiest and noblest of prophecies, that path had now to be trodden every step in agony and shame, disgrace and sorrow. He knew it all, and the remarkable thing is that though the King appeared so utterly simple and unkingly, according to the notions that men have of royalty, and although He anticipated that before Him lay the path that conducted straight to the fatal cross, yet I suppose never in all His discourses did He speak so frequently of the kingdom. These words constantly come back to that familiar note—the kingdom. The sixteenth verse, "I will not any more eat thereof, until it be fulfilled in the kingdom of God"; and "I will not drink of the fruit of the vine, until the kingdom of God shall come"; and again, "The kings of the Gentiles exercise lordship over them, . . . but ye shall not be so . . ."; and "I appoint unto you a kingdom as My Father hath appointed Me."

He knew He had His hand upon the kingdom. At first sight there seems such a striking distinction and contrast between His suffering and the kingdom. The kingdom had already been appointed. The kingdom had been appropriated before the foundation of the world, had been ratified by the promises which had been so constantly spoken to the prophets and inspired seers, and it was still to be declared when God raised Him to His right hand in the heavenly places and said, "Rule Thou in the midst of Thine enemies." Yet, though it had been so distinctly predetermined and appointed, Christ had to take a certain path by which it had to be acquired. That acquisition had to be wrought out through the cross, through suffering and pain and anguish, even to death. And so not only with Christ, but with the apostles, and with the Church, there is only one way by which the predestined, the appropriated kingdom can be acquired.

A throne is of value to a man simply in proportion of the power it gives him to elevate other men. There are certain things which are accessories to a throne, and other things which are essential to it. Amid the accessories there is the adulation of courtiers, there is abundant wealth, there are all the insignia of power. These are not worthy of our thought. I speak simply of the essentials. First, then, a throne is raised three or four feet above the floor on which other men stand, that the occupant of the throne may with greater purchase reach down to help those who are struggling to attain a place beside him. If a man is drowning in a torrent, I like to be above the torrent bed, that I might lean over to the man and help him. A throne has elevating power in it; and the only reason why Christ cares for the throne, or the apostles need boast of the throne, or the Church need envy a throne, is because it gives every one who occupies it the power to lift men. The throne has lifting power; the King is the Saviour, the kingdom means the elevation and the salvation of the world.

Now, if these premises be granted, let us quietly study Christ's path to His throne. We want to see the path by which Jesus Christ went to His throne, where He sits to-day, the ever blessed, the ever mighty Son of God. There are along the path temptation—"Ye are they which have continued with me in my temptations"; suffering—"I have desired to eat this Passover with you before I suffer"; service—"I am among you as He that serveth."

First, temptation. Just as a man climbing a hill will sit for a moment fixing his glance upon the path which he has trodden before he makes the final climb to the summit, so did Christ look back, and, lo! all the pathway had been flecked with the blood of many a conflict.

How He suffered during the thirty years spent in Nazareth we do not know, but He was tempted in all points like as we are, yet without sin. But when He emerged from the quietude of His life in Nazareth the full blast of temptation burst upon Him of Satanic hate; and upon the Mount of Temptation He met in three successive temptations the devil, who urged Him to use His God-given power for selfish purposes, to presume upon God's promises (which was a reaction of the former), and, thirdly, that by one act of wrong He might be unselfish enough to save a world; that by one act of obedience to Satan he might get the power that Satan professed to be able to give over the entire world, that, in any case, He should evade the cross. Apparently all through His life that was the one great temptation suggested to Him, because some months before He died, when Peter said, "Spare Thyself, spare Thyself, do not do it, do not think of it," Christ turned sharply to him and said, "That is what Satan is saying to me all the time. Get thee behind Me, thou who speaketh with his voice. I will not listen to thee, for this temptation is the one above all things that cuts Me to the heart."

You see, as a Man, He was so successful in His earthly career. He gathered the people together, He influenced them so widely; He was able to teach the crowds, to heal the sick; and it seemed, judging by earthly human standards, such a pity that one doing so much good should throw away His life upon the cross, and Satan kept on saying to Him, "Keep on doing as Thou art doing; go on teaching; go on healing; go on blessing men." That was the one great temptation that came to Him as He passed through life. Satan is always saying the same: "save yourself, do not cut off the flower of your youth; do not risk the danger and fever of foreign lands. Spare yourself." That was the one temptation presented to Christ, to His apostles, and to ourselves. But Jesus Christ conquered the temptation.

I suppose that was really the agony of Gethsemane, the conflict which culminated on the cross, when His faith in the Father enabled Him to pour out His soul unto death, believing that God would give Him another life. It was through this temptation that Jesus Christ quelled the power of the tempter. "Now shall the prince of this world be cast out." It was by temptation that Christ showed Himself superior, it was by temptation that our Lord's own power to sympathize with men became so vastly extended; and it was only through temptation, because He proved Himself greater than the prince of the power of the air and of the world that He was raised far above principalities and powers, to His seat at the right hand of the Father. Temptation was one part of the pathway to His throne.

And you will notice also close on that there came His sufferings, and when He speaks about His intention to suffer, you must for a moment conceive of it thus: There stood an open door, apparently open, on the Transfiguration Mount, when He might have returned with Moses

141

and Elias to His Father, just as some of those who live until He comes will be caught up, transfigured, into the air, not seeing death. But though there stood an open door and joy through which hands beckoned Him and voices called Him, he deliberately turned His back on it, and instead of taking the joy set before Him He took the path that led down into the grim valley, and deliberately, we are told, set His face to go to Jerusalem, that He might suffer, and it was through this extreme suffering, voluntarily endured, that He passed to His crown.

Mark that; there is the difference between the martyr and the Saviour. The martyr suffers, and we admire his endurance and patience. When we see John Huss suffering at the stake, how greatly it excites our pity and tender sympathy. But, then, Huss could not help it. The martyr is dragged to his death, he goes to it perhaps seeing it is inevitable, with fixed and steadfast courage. The Saviour, on the other hand, could avoid it. What distinguishes the sufferings of Christ from all others lies in the fact that they were evitable, they were avoidable, they were voluntarily assumed; that He stood at the stake bound to it by no hands but His own; that He was nailed to the cross not by the nails, but by his own fixed purpose; that He bowed His head, and breathed out His Spirit as a voluntary act. And it was just because He could suffer with completest love that He can reign over all hearts for ever. That supreme masterpiece of love will conquer, shall conquer all rebel wills, and as they say in heaven, Thou art worthy to take the books and open the seals, for Thou hast revealed to us God by Thy blood. Because He descended, He ascended; because He is supreme lover, he is the supreme Ruler and Saviour; because He went down to the darkness He is risen up into the light, and thus through His suffering,

142

as well as through His temptation, He has passed to His throne in heaven.

And then service. "I am among you as He that serveth." What wondrous service here! Among ourselves we expect a king to be served; here the King serves. We look for the insignia royal to the crown; here is a towel round His waist; the disciples sit, while He rises from supper and girds Himself with a towel and begins to wash the feet of His disciples. And that is what He has been doing ever since. "I am among you," He said, "as He that serveth." Do you not realize that Jesus Christ is still the greatest servant of the Church of the Universe? He is always getting great commissions to execute. He is always washing our feet and cleansing our hearts and attending to our wants, listening to our prayers and carrying on the great purposes of God. The whole universe is dependent upon His constant perfect ministry, and it is because Jesus Christ is the Supreme Minister of the Universe that He is Supreme Ruler of the kingdom of this world. How inevitable it is, then, that Christ should be a King, because He has mastered the power of temptation by Satan, because He loves and suffers so supremely, because He serves so absolutely, and because He perpetuates all these; for I believe in my heart of hearts that the Gospels are but a page out of the diary of His life, and that He is always overcoming Satan, that He is always suffering, that He is always serving. It is because He is all these in supreme sense evermore that He is bound to conquer, and that ultimately all the power of Satan's sin will be quelled by love. How often have I seen in these very streets working men who have given their hearts to God under my ministry, but whose wives were intolerant and hateful, persecuting them,

143

hiding their tools, making home miserable, and yet these men by patient well-doing have finally conquered their wives' hostility, and the women have ultimately come with their husbands to sit down at the Lord's Table perfectly reformed. And what love does in a home like that, the love of Christ will do in the whole universe, and He is bound to conquer.

Now, what is true of the Lord Jesus Christ was also true of the apostles. You remember the story in which two of them came and asked if they would sit beside Him in His kingdom. The Lord Jesus Christ did not say them Nay, but He said they must pay the price. Those who are to stand side by side with Him in regnant power must be prepared to be with Him, to continue with Him in His temptations. You must be baptized with the baptism wherewith He was baptized, and you must drink of His cup.

And how well it was He said that; because if you compare carefully the Gospels together, you will find that probably within a day or two of James and John making that request they were asking the Lord to allow them to call down fire from heaven to burn up a village of the Samaritans. He might well say, "Ye know not what spirit ye are of." Yesterday you asked to sit on My throne; to-day I see what power you will exert from My throne, you would call down lightning and thunder to blast the foe. Ah! said He, "Ye know not what spirit ye are of." You must pass through Calvary, you must drink of My cup, you must be baptized with My baptism, then you will lose your desire to call for thunder and lightning to blast men; the kingdom of power will come upon you—the power of the Holy Ghost—and ye shall be My witnesses.

144

A Kingdom for You

The remarkable thing is that you read in the eighth chapter of Acts that those very men went down to this very village of the Samaritans which they had wanted to blast with fire, and prayed for them that they might receive the Holy Ghost. You understand from that what the discipline of Calvary and Gethsemane, and the agony of suspense, and the forty days and ten days more, had done for these men; you see how the quality of their soul had been improved, and how they were fitted now to rule. They prayed for them, and they received the Holy Ghost. Instead of asking for thunder and lightning and power, they gave the fire of Pentecost.

There were, as you know, three groups of apostles. There was the Boanerges group of four, with Peter at the head; there was the reflective group of four, with Philip at the head; there was the practical group of four, with James at the head. Just twelve men, grouped in three groups of four each. To each of them was appointed a kingdom, but they had to win it not by calling down fire from heaven, but by temptation, suffering, service. Judas, somehow, missed it. The kingdom was appointed, but he did not acquire it, and the vacant throne had to be given to another. And Peter, to whom the same kingdom was appointed, nearly missed it. He lost his footing, and if the Lord had not caught him in the nick of time, he never would have reached his throne. But the outstretched hand of Jesus brought him back in tears, and restored him by the Lake of Galilee. And the rest, too, as they pursued the track were tempted likewise.

As to their sufferings, need I recite to you the story of their early tribulation and persecution and pain? And for service—these very apostles, let them tell the story of their remarkable services to the world, and what is the result? "I saw the new Jerusalem coming down from God out of heaven, and the wall of the city had twelve foundations, garnished with all manner of precious stones, and in the foundations the names of the twelve apostles of the Lamb." That was their kingdom; instead of being at the top of it, they were at the bottom. That, after all, is the supreme power of the man away out of sight, forgotten, ignored—just as we ignore all the systems of sewers, gullies and corridors, the gas, and electric lighting, and telephonic apparatus that underlie the city of London as we go hurrying to and fro, backwards and forwards; and yet these all help to conserve our health and our civilization. So it is, with the supreme life. The men who are tempted and who resist, the men who sorrow and suffer, the men that serve, they lie in the great slabs of jewels underneath the New Jerusalem; and they who go to and fro the golden streets hardly realize how the city came to be so fair. They know not all that lies unseen, recognized only by God. That is the way the twelve apostles of the Lamb are ruling.

And what is true thus of Christ and of the apostles is true also of the Church. There are not many soft places to the feet. For the most part, cliffs have to be climbed with cut and bleeding feet. That is one path of the Church, and if you look back you notice all along through the centuries a continuous story of temptation, under which too often the Church has succumbed, for she unlike her Lord, has worshipped circumstance and power, that she may get dominion and empire in the world. Through temptation, through suffering, the sufferings of our own martyrs here in our own country, the sufferings of martyrs throughout the missionary world—this is the Church's contribution to the world. Often it lies hidden, like the jewels beneath the New Jerusalem. The

146

Church's work underpins the civilization which is springing up throughout the world; for the only civilization which is permanent is that which is based upon the previous work of the Church.

And what is true of the Church is true of each one of us. Every time being tempted we overcome, every time we persevere through suffering for others, every time we serve with humility and lowliness, we approach nearer and nearer to the throne, because the marvellous point is that whereas earthly thrones are ascended, we descend to heavenly thrones. We go up, up, in this world to the throne; we go down, down, in the other world. The man who will go down lowest, and quickest, and furthest, is the man who has supreme power. And the result is certain. Our point is the kingdom.

The waves flow to ebb, advance to recede, break in foam on their way, and often we think they are tired and make no inch of progress; but we forget that the kingdom is appointed; away back at the heart of God there is the eternal purpose, and from the heart of the infinite God the mighty tide is setting which has yet to carry forward hatred, cruelty, violence, excess, sensuality, and to sweep these all away. The kingdom is appointed, but we must abide with Jesus through this little time of temptation, suffering, and service, that we may acquire that kingdom.

A GOOD MOTTO FOR HAPPY LIVING

"For thine is the kingdom, and the power, and the glory for ever. Amen."

MATTHEW 6:13

IS IT POSSIBLE FOR US to have a motto which shall more exactly work out in a noble life than this threefold motto? For if the kingdom of your heart is God's, and if the power of your life by which you realize your ideals is God's, and if the motive and purpose of your life be for the greater glory of God, I think you have got everything there that will make your life a strong, sweet and blessed one.

"Thine is the kingdom." Not Thine shall be the kingdom. To me there is little doubt that the kingdom is here. I base that upon those words of our Lord: "There are some standing here who shall not taste of death until they see the Son of Man coming in His kingdom." Evidently our Lord meant that some would taste of death before the kingdom came. The Transfiguration took place within a few days, and it is not probable that before then any died out of that little group that stood around Him; therefore, we cannot suppose that the promise of our Lord was fulfilled in the Transfiguration. On the other hand, we know a great many did die before; but a few survived to see the fall of Jerusalem in the year 70. My belief is that that was one of the greatest epochs in the world's story; that then the Hebrew epoch or age came to a close, and the Kingdom of God was erected or constituted. Therefore those parables in Matthew 13, in which our Lord speaks of the Kingdom of Heaven, seem to me to be the story of the age in which we ourselves are living, during which He is taking out of His kingdom

151

all things that offend and work iniquity, and is bringing that kingdom into manifestation. The kingdom is here.

I am quite aware that there is a great revolt, but that does not hinder the fact that the kingdom has come. You will remember that David was God's constituted king, and he set up his kingdom over Israel. Absalom, his ne'er-do-well son, gathered to himself the hearts of the men of Israel and cajoled them, pretending he would do better for them than his father did. "Oh! that I were made judge in the land," he said, "that every man which hath any suit or cause might come unto me, and I would do him justice," Absalom stole away the hearts of the men of Israel, but David was still God's king, and those who gathered round him might have said, "Thine, O David, is the kingdom. Absalom has come into Jerusalem, and holds it; but thine, O son of Jesse, is the kingdom. Absalom may gather the men of Israel as the sand on the seashore in order to uphold his power, but it will crumble, for thine, O David, is the kingdom." And presently Absalom's power does crumble, and David comes to his own. So I believe—and the longer I think about it the more sure I am—that Jesus Christ is God's designated King of men, and that just as in the conservatoire of music, amid all the scales and the mistakes and the efforts of those who wish to become pianists, there stands erected the true conception and ideal of music, that the discords will presently die out and the kingdom of music will become manifested; and just as in the Royal Academy there may be many pictures absolutely unworthy of being put on the walls, but amid all the failures and shortcomings there always stands the majestic kingdom of beauty; and just as amid all the lies that are being told by men, told on the public platform, told through the Press, told in literature— nevertheless there stands the kingdom of absolute truth before which all these lies will some day pass as froth upon the ocean; so I believe, unseen by the eye of the ordinary man, there is standing among us the Kingdom of Christ, of which Christ is the head, and whose legislation was laid down in the Sermon on the Mount.

For never forget the kingdom is the Divine order of human society. Just as when we were boys and girls we looked at our copy-books and saw our poor, uneven hand-writing underneath the copper-plate at the top of the page, so amid all the lies and changes and revolutions of earth there is God's kingdom, now a mystery, that will some day be revealed. Because it is there the order of society is maintained.

Where does society come from? Do you think society came out of the brain of man? Do you think we owe it to Plato or to Moses? To neither of these ultimately, but to Plato and Moses reading from the eternal tablets of God's constitution all those mighty conceptions of government which are for ever associated with their name. And just as underneath this body of yours and mine there is forming an eternal body in which the soul will robe itself when at death it passes forth, and the presence of that body beneath this changing dust keeps the form, keeps the figure, keeps the general appearance of the face the same, so under all the shifting and changing of human life and society there is a Divine order. Revolution will expend itself in vain, and mankind will never go back to chaos, because underneath all government and the power of judge and constable there lie the great outlines of the Kingdom of God. The Christian man is bound to be a politician because he sees the outlines of that kingdom, and is constantly desiring to write the statutes of that kingdom upon the statute book of his fatherland. Ever

since I saw the kingdom I could not help being a politician.
I do not mean a party politician; but I have striven in my
humble way to translate that which I see—the Kingdom
of God—and make it operative among nations and com-
munities of men. If God's is the kingdom, He will take
you in His care, and He will bring you presently to that
refreshing, soul-restoring water. Be calm and still. God
is King. He will find your niche in the kingdom. He will
bring you to the open door. He will bring you your
chance. Over every young man who has been daunted
and disappointed, but who still grips his sword with
unconquerable courage, God the Father is bending.
"Thine is the kingdom."

It may be necessary for you to wait in the shadow,
to stand on sentry duty, and only at the last hour of
your life may you be allowed to rush into the fray, and
with a few minutes of fighting end your career. "Thine
is the kingdom." Oh, believe in God. Believe that, above
all, there is an eternal program; that above your employ-
ers, above those who are constantly watching you to see
whether you do your duty, amid all the chaos of daily
life eddying round you, God has a program and God has
a plan, and God has a purpose. He has assigned places
to us. Life is a Divine thought which we have to work
out. Oh, sing it, chant it, whisper it to your heart, you
who feel baffled and disappointed—say, in spite of it all,
"Thine, O my Father, is the kingdom."

And "Thine is the power." Is it not exquisitely beautiful that this comes at the end of the prayer? "Hallowed
be Thy name." . . . "Thine is the power"—to secure its
hallowing. "Thy kingdom come." . . . "Thine is the
power"—to bring it into evidence. "Give us this day our
daily bread." . . . "Thine is the power"—to make the

ravens bring it, or to make the handful of meal last out, to make the little money you have last until you get a situation. "Forgive us our trespasses and help us to forgive others." . . . "Thine is the power"—to make these hard hearts gentle. "Lead us not into temptation." . . . "Thine is the power" against which the adversary will break his bows in vain. "Deliver us from evil," because Thine is the power to do it. Oh, at the close of every petition, stay for a little while and rest upon that Selah. "Thine is the power" by which this petition of mine may be brought to pass.

The millionaire says, "Mine is the power," but his money perishes. The orator says, "Mine is the power," but his vocal cords fail him. The artist says, "Mine is the power to bewitch and entrance men," but his hand is paralyzed. Nothing in this world is so disappointing as the boast of power. We find ourselves able to do so little. The things which we think are so big do not last; the most enormous exertions yield so small a result. Weaker men appear to do things we cannot touch. People whom we despise, whom we count as ciphers, who seem to have such meagre resources, are able to achieve so much in the world; while we men of genius, men of birth, men who ought to have power, have not got it. Life is full of instances of that kind. But it is a great thing when a man realizes that power belongs to God, and when he realizes himself to be a medium through which God's power operates.

There is nothing you cannot do if you learn that; if you once believe that as the pen in Milton's hand conveyed Milton's power to the page, and through the page to generations; and as the power in Raphael's wrist passed into his brush, and through that brush to the canvas, so if you really want to bring about the kingdom of God on earth, the kingdom of truth, beauty, and love, you need only yield your life to God; and if you desire in your heart only the glory of God, you will find the power of God begin to thrill through you like the electricity in the wires which act as a medium for conveying power to these electric lamps. The millionaire, the artist, the literary man who boasts of his power often shuts himself off from the source of power. Everything in this world depends upon whether a man works for God, or allows God to work through him.

A great evangelist, Dr. Chapman, has often told a story about myself and himself. He had been in business, and became minister of a great church in Philadelphia. One Monday he was more than usually dispirited. The Sunday had been a poor one, and he felt, as we ministers often feel, as if he could never preach again. He had sat down at his desk and written his resignation, and was intending to post it to his church officers, when a girl brought in *The New York Tribune,* containing an address I had delivered on the previous Friday at Northfield. In that address I said what I have said to you, that it is not what a man does for God that tells, but what God does through human life. Dr. Chapman was arrested by that. He knelt down and said: "O God, I have worked for Thee, and have failed. Now work through me." And he said to himself, "If God does things through me, and I yield myself to Him, there is no limit to the possibilities of my life." He rose up, tore up the letter, and resumed his pastorate, and since then he has gone on from strength to strength.

And "Thine is the glory." If you seek your own glory you will lose that, and His. But if you seek His, you will get yours. We are all tempted, like the youth Narcissus in the Greek fable, to bend over the brook and fall in love with ourselves, and we get changed into flowers, and fade in an hour. But he that doeth the will of God, and seeketh the will of God, abideth for ever. When men compliment you upon the excellence of your character, and tell you how spiritual you are, and how sweet is your influence, say, Thine is the glory, O Christ; I have got it all from Thee. If you write a book—"Thine is the glory" on the frontispiece. If you paint a picture—"Thine is the glory" as a scroll at the foot. If you are a doctor or a surgeon, and are able to render some great service of deliverance, do not take thanks without in your heart saying, "Thine is the glory." I like to think of those angels standing before God and praising Him day and night—angels excelling in strength, doing His commandments, hearkening to His voice; I like to think of them traveling through the realms of space, and making them the home of song; I like to think of them reaching the far distance where the ether breaks upon the rocks of eternity, and in that far distant land saying, "Glory to God! Glory to God in the highest."

Is not this, then, the motto that we want? Is it not something to live for? Thine is the kingdom over men, and over my life. Thine is the power and the glory. Will you all dare to say, "For ever, Amen"? Will you not at this very moment say in your heart, Jesus, my King, rule over me? He died for you. He loves you. He can bless you. Will you now put the crown of your life upon Him?

THE MIND OF CHRIST

"Let this mind be in you, which was also in Christ Jesus."

PHILIPPIANS 2:5

IT IS OUR DUTY to build our human life upon the Divine pattern. "See," said God to Moses, "that thou make all things after the pattern shown on the Mount." It is on the mount with God that a man gets his true conception of how to build on earth. Think over the thoughts of Christ. Get away from the low levels of life and stand face to face with the Son of God. Think as Christ thought. Think, think over again the very thoughts that occupied the mind of Christ when He made that stupendous stoop from the dignity of the Throne to the degradation of the pit. Kepler, the first of great modern astronomers, said, as he turned his early telescope to the nebulae, "I am thinking over again the first, the earliest thoughts of God."

We are told, first, that Jesus Christ was in the form of God, and the grammarian tells us that this stands for "essence of God," and whatever God Himself is in His infinite essence—omnipotent, omnipresent, omniscient, the Eternal—that also was Jesus Christ. He was in the bosom of God. From eternal ages He was God, and whatever we predicate of God the Father we must also predicate of Jesus Christ our Lord. Men sometimes find fault with us because we hold the Trinity in unity; and yet the man who thinks thus does not thoroughly understand his own nature, for what is any person here but a trinity in unity? For surely spirit and body blend in one personality. Besides, you cannot speak of God as being loved without implicating the Trinity. For if there be love there must be at least twain, one to love and one to be loved. And if God is love, He must have had a Son whom He should love, and there must be the spirit of union between the two, and you cannot, therefore, utter that wonderful definition of St. John, "God is love," without implicating the Divine Trinity, and without affirming over again what my text says, that Jesus Christ was in the form of God. He was in the form of God, but we are told, He thought it not robbery to be God's equal. Or the Greek is, He thought it not a thing to grasp at to be God's equal. When a woman is not sure that her husband loves her, she is always grasping at his love, laying traps for him, always proud to show her lady friends that in this or that he has not failed her. She is always so eager and careful to elicit his love, to prove it. Now, there was no need for Jesus Christ to do so; it was universally conceded. He thought it not robbery to be equal with God, nor a thing to be grasped at, because the highest archangels who stood around His throne acknowledged it, and all through His life He constantly bore witness to it. Remember how in the society of His intimates He said, "We will come and make our abode with him"—My Father and I, classing Himself with God the Father in the same pronoun "We." You will remember how also in public He said, "I and My Father are One"; and when He stood at the court of Caiaphas, He said, "You shall see me seated in the clouds and coming in my Father's glory," for He thought it not robbery to occupy the throne of the Eternal and to robe Himself in His Deity. And you will remember also when He was dying—for death strips us of all pretense and sham—He took the key and opened the gate of Paradise to the dead malefactor, for He did not think it robbery to share the prerogative of forgiveness with the Father. All through His life the self-consciousness of Jesus Christ is the main argument in His Deity. He was proved to be the Son of God by the resurrection from the dead; He has proved to be the Son of God by the testimony of history; but to my mind He is most proved to be the Son of God by His own self-consciousness; He bore Himself as such, and though He were the humblest and meekest of mankind He never counted it robbery to claim equality with God.

But my text descends. He was in the form of man, but thought it not robbery to be equal with God. He emptied Himself for us, so the Greek runs. George Herbert, in his quaint and poetic manner, tries to make out that all the while that Jesus Christ stooped downwards to our earth He was divesting Himself of the splendor of His Divine appearance. Says George Herbert, "He laid aside His crown, and became the stars of the Milky Way; He put down His sceptre, and it became the lightning flash; He put aside His robe, and it became the clouds of amber at sunset or sunrise; He stripped Himself of His girdle, and it became the rainbow that arches the sky." Ah, that is poetic; but there is something deeper than this which I need to bring you to, that you may understand the deep meaning and significance and fitness of this passage. He emptied Himself surely of the use of His Divine attributes; and just as I might wish to live my human life holding my right hand behind my back, though at any moment able to avail myself of it, but trying to do what I have to do year after year with my left hand, so Jesus Christ stooped to

163

our world, voluntarily laying aside the use of His Divine attributes that He might live a truly human life as man, and overcome the power of the devil. Of course God could quench the devil. Of course, with one stroke of His Divine power the devil would be bruised under His feet; but that would not have been, so to speak, fair; that would not have vindicated God's original creation of human nature, and therefore, in the person of His Son, the Eternal God, denying the use of His Divine attributes for the moment, lived a truly human life, emptying Himself.

I know in earlier life I thought that the miracle of the quelling of the storm, or of the raising of the dead, or of the healing of the leper, were indications of the inherent power that dwelt in the nature of Christ. I think more accurately, I trust, now, as I realize that He shows how to live the life of unutterable dependence on the infinite power of God, the same life that you and I have to live, in Himself, and that the power which resided in Him was the power that He took moment by moment from God. Let me illustrate that so that the simplest person in my audience may understand, because to understand this is not only to understand the mystery of the Incarnation, but to understand also the Gospel by St. John. Not to understand this is to miss the true standard of vision.

Suppose I was born in Paris, and that therefore I have a perfect knowledge of the English tongue from my parents, and of the French tongue by my education. I talk to my French nurse from the earliest in French. I grow to manhood, I remove to London. I have a home of my own, and my own little child presently begins to learn French. I find her troubling and stammering over the vocabulary and the grammar, the pronunciation and the exercises. Supposing by a voluntary act I was able to shut off that department of my brain in which the knowledge of the French language resides—not an impossible supposition, mark you, because those who have suffered from concussion of the brain will remember that during the hours that that concussion lasted we lost all consciousness of a good many departments of knowledge, while we retained others. We will suppose, then, that voluntarily I am able to shut off my knowledge of the French language, and I sit by my little girl's side, and I spell out to her the first difficult lessons of the French language. And as month succeeds to month, and year to year, I presently come to know French with my child, and we stand together as perfect French scholars. Supposing, then, that I take back to my life the knowledge that I had of French by my birth, do you not see that I should have a double source of power. I should understand French now as I learned it, but I should know French also as I had acquired it; and just as in the northern sky, at midsummer, upon the same clouds blend the rays of sunrise and of sunset at the dying of the day, so in me would blend the double knowledge of French. That seems to me an exact parallel. My Saviour, that He might know my human life, that He might know what conflict and temptation are, that He might be able to be an example in whose steps I should follow, laid aside the immediate use of the attributes of His Deity, and, emptying Himself of it, came to be as men are, as I am, sin excepted. But when He rose, and went through yon sky, He passed the door, and said, "Glorify Thou me with the glory that I had with Thee before the world was made." So that in Him to-day there blend the lives of the perfect servant and of the Eternal God. He emptied Himself.

And do you not see that in every human life there comes a similar emptying. Let me tell you for a moment an illustrative incident. Tauler, who was almost contemporary with Luther, was one of the greatest orators of his time, a man deeply and wondrously eloquent, and whenever he mounted his pulpit at Strasburg Cathedral it was crowded with all sorts and conditions of men, from the mayor downwards. And across the hills of Switzerland there came Nicholas, the Switzer. He sat amid the crowd, and found his way to Tauler. He said "I want to confess to you." "Certainly," said Tauler. But after the first confession Tauler found that it was he who needed to confess, rather than Nicholas. He told Nicholas that his life was a failure, that beneath the outward splendor of it there was a hungry heart. He had not found the pivot, the center of rest, and he said, "What must I do?" "You must die, Master Tauler." "Die?" said he. "Ah, ah, you will never get the true source of power till you have died to your own." And for a year the pulpit missed the great preacher, and in his soul he was empty of all faith in his eloquence and learning, and became but a little child. And again he went back to his pulpit, and the place was crowded again, and five minutes after he started preaching he broke down and buried his face in absolute confusion; and the people, as they passed out disappointed said, "Our great preacher is spoiled." And then he began simply and talked to the poor people that gathered round him once or twice in the church, and the fame of it spread, and those sermons were preached, sermons which the heart of man will never allow to die until sin and sorrow have fled away for ever. Don't you see how sometimes it is necessary for a man to empty himself even as Christ did, of his reliance upon his native power, that being as a little child he may get power back from God after another sort.

"He stops to heal the woman"

The Mind of Christ

Have you ever thought of the two mountains in our Savior's life? There was the mountain of Temptation, when the devil offered Him all the kingdoms of the world in a moment of time if He would only worship him. And on it all Christ turned His back; He was not going to use His Divine power to help Himself, and He was not going to yield to the devil's temptation. And He passed through death down into death, and passing through death, He stood upon the Mount of Ascension and said, "All power is given to Me in heaven and upon earth." And so in our life and in yours you may depend upon it that there will come times in which God takes the soul aside, strips it and empties it, and its self-reliance is at an end, and lying down helplessly before God, God takes it up, and out of such a death there comes life to millions. He emptied Himself.

Again, He took upon Himself the form of a servant, the form of a slave, one of unutterable obedience. The life of Jesus Christ was one of such perfect obedience that He was always shaping His life upon the pattern which God had set. I am very deeply wrought whenever I think of this. Of course illustrations of it are infinite in our Saviour's life. For instance, Jairus comes to ask Him to heal his child, and Christ goes to heal his daughter, and suddenly He feels a minute touch, so delicate that it was almost insensible, the touch of a withered hand, and immediately He lays aside His plan of raising the daughter of Jairus, because He has caught sight of an intricacy in His Father's plans, and He stops to heal the woman, even though it leads to His being too late to save the life of a little girl. That is one instance out of many of the absolute obedience that Christ gave to

167

His Father's will. And you will find that that is the only way to live, to do this thing because God calls for it. And He calls for it in the circumstances of your life. It is a very little thing. You say, "My life is all bits and tags, it is all odds and ends; if only I had some great thing to do there would be something to show, but I am always kept doing this." Yes, be obedient. Whenever the woman touches you with her wasted hand, stop. Whenever the father comes to you about his daughter, go. Whenever there is some altercation which needs your soothing hand, smooth it out. Keep doing little things; obey; be obedient, obedient to God's calling and circumstances; and when you lie down in your dying bed you will say to yourself, "Well, there is not much to show." But when you get up in heaven God will take your hand and say, "Come with Me, I want to show you something." And He will lead you to a place where you and He will be utterly alone, and He will unfold something to you; He will lift up the veil and show you a beautiful thing, a lovely fabric. And you will say, "What is that?" And God will say, "Don't you know what it is?" And you will say, "No, I don't indeed." God will say, "That is your life." "My life? But I only spent my life in doing odds and ends." And God will say, "See, I took those odds and ends and built them up into this. Here it is." And it will be a Gospel. You see these Gospels are only the result of Christ doing little things as they came across His path, and they were woven by God's Spirit into the Gospel. And your life will be a gospel if you will obey the call of circumstance, which is the call of God. He became obedient.

And it also says, fifthly, that He took upon Him the

form of a servant, was made in the likeness of men. I like to think of Jesus Christ as the little baby that suckled at Mary's breast, playing with the shavings in the carpenter's shop, set up against the wall to have its first essay in walking, and Mary, with her arms outstretched to catch Him as He fell; growing up as a boy to take such interest in the lilies, in the birds on their flight to their nests at night, and in all the wonderful life of Nature, sitting in the village synagogue and listening to the Law, but never dreaming that the light which woke upon the Law was borrowed from His boy's face; going for the first time to the Temple, and looking at the wonderful and glorious city and the Temple of marble, and then afterwards passing through just the very phases of manhood which we all pass, and knowing so truly and absolutely what manhood was. It is such a relief to me to realize that it was not simply God in the phase of our humanity, but that, somehow, God Himself stepped into our world and wept our tears and bore our sorrows and met our temptations and died our death, and that He who was perfect Man was also perfect God. He came down to this, and this was low enough; but I think the fifth point is the most wonderful: that He became obedient to death; the Commander in Chief doffed His helmet to one of His own officers; He became obedient to death. He need not have died. The first man need not have died; he was deathless so long as he remained sinless; sin brought death. Jesus did not sin, therefore Jesus need not have died. And I always think that when He stood upon the Mount of Transfiguration, and the door was opened through which Moses and Elijah had come, and the radiance was streaming through, had our Saviour chosen He might have stepped back with them.

169

But a long way down through the cypress grove there stood the cross. He did not want to be the patron, He desired to be the Saviour of men, and so turned His back upon the radiant glory and His face towards the cross; He became obedient unto death.

When I was in Canterbury Cathedral, about fifteen years ago, it was different to what it is to-day. I had visited the floor of the church, and the sacristan asked me if I desired to see the crypt, the hidden place; and I told him I would see everything there was to see. He said, "You will find it down there, sir." There was a sort of circular hole in the tesselated floor, and an iron railing and a spiral staircase. But it was so dark, and the smell of corruption was so great that my heart misgave me, and I wished I had never said I would descend. But I did. I put my hand upon the rail, and I went round and round, and every time I put my foot down I did not know where it would rest. I got down step by step until I stood on a pavement. And I looked under the church, and at the far end a wide door was opened into the cloister garden, and the fountain was flashing in the light of a June day, and the flowers were all in their loveliness and fragrance, and I saw that a man has to go down the crypt to come out into the garden. And I remembered that text that said in the place where Jesus was crucified there was a garden. And it seemed to me as though I knew what He must have felt when, in Gethsemane, He put His hand upon the iron rail of His Father's will and began to descend, singing as He went, "Thou wilt not leave My soul in Hades, neither wilt Thou suffer Thy beloved One to see corruption. Thou shalt show Me the Path of Life; in Thy presence is the fulness of joy."

It is only through death that you will reach your true

life; it is only through what the world calls failure that you will touch your truest success. It is only when you have fallen on the ground to die that you cannot die alone.

THE SECRET OF HIS PRESENCE

"Thou shalt hide them in the secret of thy presence."

PSALM 31:20

IN ONE SENSE GOD is always near us. He is not an Absentee, needing to be brought down from the heavens or up from the deep. He is nigh at hand. His Being pervades all being. Every world, that floats like an islet in the ocean of space, is filled with signs of His presence, just as the home of your friend is littered with the many evidences of his residence, by which you know that he lives there, though you have not seen his face. Every crocus pushing through the dark mould; every fire-fly in the forest; every bird that springs up from its nest before your feet; everything that is—*all* are as full of God's presence, as the bush which burned with His fire, before which Moses bared his feet in acknowledgment that God was there.

But we do not always realize it. We often pass hours, and days, and weeks; we sometimes engage in seasons of prayer; we go to and fro from His house, where the ladder of communion rests; and still He is a shadow, a name, a tradition, a dream of days gone by.

"Oh! that I know where I might find Him, that I might come even to His seat. Behold! I go forward, but He is not there; and backward but I cannot perceive Him; on the left hand, where He doth work, but I cannot behold Him; He hideth Himself on the right hand, and I see Him not."

How different is this failure to realize the presence of God to the blessed experience of His nearness realized by some.

Brother Lawrence, the simple-minded cook, tells us that for more than sixty years he never lost the sense of the presence of God, but was as conscious of it while

175

performing the duties of his humble office, as when partaking of the Holy Supper.

John Howe, on the blank page of his Bible, made this record in Latin: "This very morning I awoke out of a most ravishing and delightful dream, when a wonderful and copious stream of celestial rays, from the lofty throne of the Divine Majesty, seemed to dart into my open and expanded breast. I have often since reflected on that very signal pledge of special Divine favor, and have with repeated fresh pleasure tasted the delights thereof."

Another experience is recorded thus: "Suddenly there came on my soul a something I had never known before. It was as if some One Infinite and Almighty, knowing everything, full of the deepest, tenderest interest in myself, made known to me that He loved me. My eye saw no one, but I knew assuredly that the One whom I knew not, and had never met, had met me for the first time, and made known to me that we were together."

Are not these experiences, so blessed and inspiring, similar to that of the author of the longest, and, in some respects, the sublimest Psalm in the Psalter? He had been beating out the golden ore of thought through successive paragraphs of marvelous power and beauty, when suddenly he seems to have become conscious that He, of whom he had been speaking, had drawn near, and was bending over him. The sense of the presence of God was borne in upon his inner consciousness. And, lifting up a face, on which reverence and ecstasy met and mingled, he cried, *"Thou art near, O Lord!"* (Ps 119:51)

If only such an experience of the nearness of God were always ours, enwrapping us as air or light; if only we could feel, as the great Apostle put it on Mars' Hill, that God is not far away, but the element in which we have our being, as sea-flowers in deep still lagoons;—

then we should understand what David meant when he
spoke about dwelling in the house of the Lord all the
days of his life, beholding His beauty, inquiring in His
temple, and hidden in the secret of His pavilion (Ps. 27).
Then, too, we should acquire the blessed secret of *peace,
purity*, and *power*.

In the Secret of His Presence there is Peace. "In the world
ye shall have tribulation," our Master said, "but in Me
ye shall have peace." It is said that a certain insect has
the power of surrounding itself with a film of air,
encompassed in which it drops into the midst of muddy,
stagnant pools, and remains unhurt. And the believer is
also conscious that he is enclosed in the invisible film of
the Divine Presence, as a far-traveled letter in the envelope
which protects it from hurt and soil.

"They draw near me that follow after mischief," but
Thou art nearer than the nearest, and I dwell in the
inner ring of Thy presence; the mountains round about
me are filled with the horses and chariots of Thy
protection; no weapon that is formed against me can
prosper, for it can only reach me through Thee, and,
touching Thee, will glance harmlessly aside. To be in
God is to be in a well-fitted house when the storm has
slipped from its leash; or in a sanctuary, the doors of
which shut out the pursuer.

In the Secret of His Presence there is Purity. The mere
vision of snow-capped Alps, seen from afar across Geneva's
lake, so elevates and transfigures the rapt and wistful
soul as to abash all evil things which would thrust
themselves upon the inner life. The presence of a little
child, with its guileless purity, has been known to disarm
passion, as a beam of light, falling in a reptile-haunted
cave, scatters the slimy snakes. But what shall not Thy
presence do for me, if I acquire a perpetual sense of it,

177

and live in its secret place? Surely, in the heart of that fire, black cinder though I be, I shall be kept pure, and glowing, and intense!

In the Secret of His Presence there is Power. My cry, day and night, is for power—spiritual power. Not the power of intellect, oratory, or human might. These cannot avail to vanquish the serried ranks of evil. Thou sayest truly that it is not by might or power. Yet human souls which touch Thee become magnetized, and charged with a spiritual force which the world can neither gainsay nor resist. Oh! let me touch Thee! Let me dwell in unbroken contact with Thee, that out of Thee successive tides of Divine energy may pass into and through my emptied and eager spirit, flowing, but never ebbing, and lifting me into a life of blessed ministry, which shall make deserts like the garden of the Lord.

But how shall we get and keep this sense of God's nearness? Must we go back to Bethel, with its pillar of stone, where even *Jacob* said, "Surely God is in this place?" Ah, we might have stood beside him, with unanointed eye, and seen no ladder, heard no voice; while the patriarch would discover God in the bare moorlands of our lives, trodden by us without reverence or joy. Must we travel to the mouth of the cave in whose shadow *Elijah* stood, thrilled by the music of the still small voice, sweeter by contrast with the thunder and the storm? Alas! we might have stood beside him unconscious of that glorious Presence, while Elijah, if living now, would discern it in the whisper of the wind, the babbling of babes, the rhythm of heart-throbs. If we had stationed ourselves in our present state beside the *Apostle Paul* when he was caught into the third heaven, we should probably have seen nothing but a tent-maker's shop, or a dingy room in a hired lodging. We in the dark, while he

178

was in transports. While he would discern, were he to live again, angels on our steam-ships, visions in our temples, doors opening into heaven amid the tempered glories of our more somber skies.

In point of fact we carry everywhere our circumference of light or dark. God is as much in the world as He was when Enoch walked with Him, and Moses communed with Him face to face. He is as willing to be a living, bright, glorious Reality to us as to them. But the fault is with us. Our eyes are unanointed, because our hearts are not right. The pure in heart still see God. And to those who love Him, and do His commandments, He still manifests Himself as He does not to the world. Let us cease to blame our times; let us blame ourselves. We are degenerate, not they.

What, then, is that temper of soul which most readily perceives the presence and nearness of God? Let us endeavor to learn the blessed secret of abiding ever in the secret of His Presence and of being hidden in His Pavilion (Ps. 31:20).

Remember then, at the outset, that neither thou, nor any of our race, can have that glad consciousness of the Presence of God except through Jesus. None knoweth the Father but the Son, and those to whom the Son reveals Him; and none cometh to the Father but by Him. Apart from Jesus the Presence of God is an object of terror, from which devils hide themselves in hell, and sinners weave aprons, or hide among the trees. But in Him all barriers are broken down, all veils rent, all clouds dispersed, and the weakest believer may live, where Moses sojourned, in the midst of the fire, before whose consuming flames no impurity can stand.

What part of the Lord's work is most closely connected with this blessed sense of the Presence of God?

It is through the blood of His Cross that sinners are made nigh. For in His death He not only revealed the tender love of God, but put away our sins, and wove for us those garments of stainless beauty, in which we are gladly welcomed into the inner Presence-chamber of the King. Remember it is said: "I will commune with thee from off the mercy-seat." That golden slab on which Aaron sprinkled blood whenever he entered the most Holy Place was a type of Jesus. He is the true mercy-seat. And it is when thou enterest into deepest fellowship with Him in His death, and livest most constantly in the spirit of His memorial supper, that thou shalt realize most deeply His nearness. Now, as at Emmaus, He loves to make Himself known in the breaking of bread.

And is this all? for I have heard this many times, and still fail to live in the secret place as I would.

Exactly so; and therefore, to do for us what no effort of ours could do, our Lord has received of His Father the promise of the Holy Ghost, that He should bring into our hearts the very Presence of God. Understand that since thou art Christ's, the blessed Comforter is thine. He is within thee as He was within thy Lord; and in proportion as thou dost live in the Spirit, and walk in the Spirit, and open thine entire nature to Him, thou wilt find thyself becoming His Presence-chamber, irradiated with the light of His glory. And as thou dost realize that He is in thee, thou wilt realize that thou art ever in Him. Thus the beloved Apostle wrote, "Hereby know we that we dwell in Him, and He in us, because He hath given us of His Spirit."

All this I know, and yet I fail to realize this marvelous fact of the indwelling of the Spirit in me; how then can I ever realize my indwelling in Him?

It is because thy life is so hurried; thou dost not

take time enough for meditation and prayer; the Spirit of God within thee and the Presence of God without thee cannot be discerned while the senses are occupied with pleasure, or the pulse beats quickly, or the brain is filled with the tread of many hurrying thoughts. It is when water stands that it becomes pellucid, and reveals the pebbly beach below. Be still, and know that God is within thee and around. In the hush of the soul the unseen becomes visible, and the eternal real. The eye dazzled by the sun cannot detect the beauties of its pavilion till it has had time to rid itself of the glare. Let no day pass without its season of silent waiting before God.

Are there any other conditions which I should fulfill, so that I may abide in the secret of His Presence?

"Be pure in heart." Every permitted sin encrusts the windows of the soul with thicker layers of grime, obscuring the vision of God. But every victory over impurity and selfishness clears the spiritual vision, and there fall from the eyes, as it had been, scales. In the power of the Holy Ghost deny self, give no quarter to sin, resist the devil, and thou shalt see God.

The unholy soul could not see God, even though it were set down in the midst of heaven. But holy souls see God amid the ordinary commonplaces of earth, and find everywhere an open vision. Such could not be nearer God, though they stood by the sea of glass. Their only advantage there would be that, the veil of their mortal and sinful natures having been rent, the vision would be directer and more perfect.

Keep His commandments. Let there be not one jot or tittle unrecognized and unkept. *He that hath My commandments and keepeth them, he it is that loveth Me, and he that loveth Me shall be loved of My Father, and I will love* him, and will manifest Myself to him! Moses, the faithful servant, was also the seer, and spake with God face to face as a man speaketh with his friend.

Continue in the Spirit of Prayer. Sometimes the vision will tarry to test the earnestness and steadfastness of thy desire. At other times it will come as the dawn steals over the sky, and, or ever thou art aware thou wilt find thyself conscious that He is near. He was ever wont to glide, unheralded, into the midst of His disciples through unopened doors. "Thy footsteps are not known."

At such times we may truly say with St. Bernard: "He entered not by the eyes, for His presence was not marked by color; nor by the ears, for there was no sound; nor by the breath, for He mingled not with the air; nor by the touch, for He was impalpable. You ask, then, how I knew that He was present. Because He was a quickening power. As soon as He entered, He awoke my slumbering soul; He moved and pierced my heart, which before was strange, stony, hard and sick, so that my soul could bless the Lord, and all that is within me praised His Holy Name."

Cultivate the habit of speaking aloud to God. Not, perhaps, always, because our desires are often too sacred or deep to be put into words. But it is well to acquire the habit of speaking to God as to a present friend while sitting in the house or walking by the way. Seek the habit of talking things over with God—thy letters, thy plans, thy hopes, thy mistakes, thy sorrows and sins. Things look very differently when brought into the calm light of His presence. One cannot talk long with God aloud without feeling that He is near.

Meditate much upon the Word. This is the garden where the Lord God walks, the temple where He dwells, the presence-chamber where He holds court, and is found by those who seek Him. It is through the word that we feed upon the Word. And He said: "He that eateth My flesh, and drinketh My blood, dwelleth in Me and I in him."

Be diligent in Christian work. The place of prayer is indeed the place of His manifested presence. But that presence would fade from it were we to linger there after the bell of duty had rung for us below. But we shall ever meet it as we go about our necessary work: "Thou meetest him that worketh righteousness." As we go forth to our daily tasks the angel of His presence comes to greet us, and turns to go at our side. "Go ye," said the Master. "Lo I am with you all the days." Not only in temple courts, or in sequestered glens, or in sick rooms, but in the round of daily duty, in the common-places of life, on the dead levels of existence, we may be ever in the secret of His Presence, and shall be able to say with Elijah before Ahab, and Gabriel to Zacharias, "I stand in the presence of God" (1 Kings 17:1; Luke 1:19).

Let us cultivate the habit of recognizing the Presence of God. "Blessed is the man whom Thou choosest, and causest to approach unto Thee, that He may dwell in Thy courts." There is no life like this, to feel that God is with us. That He never leads us through a place too narrow for Him to pass as well. That we can never be lonely again, never for a single moment. That we are beset by Him behind and before, and covered by His hand. That He could not be nearer to us, even if we were in heaven itself. To have Him as Friend, and Referee, and Counsellor, and Guide. To realize that there is never to be a Jericho in our lives without the presence of the Captain of the Lord's host, with those invisible but mighty legions, before whose charge all walls must fall down. What wonder that the saints of old

183

waxed valiant in fight as they heard Him say: "I am with thee; I will never leave nor forsake thee." Begone fear and sorrow and dread of the dark valley! "Thou shalt hide me in the secret of Thy Presence from the pride of man; Thou shalt keep me secretly in a pavilion from the strife of tongues."

LIVING IN THE AWARENESS OF HIS LOVE

"Keep yourselves in the love of God, looking for the mercy of our Lord Jesus Christ unto eternal life."

JUDE 21

THE LONGER WE LIVE, the less we care to speak of our love to God, and the more we dwell in God's love to us. As we climb the hill of Christian experience, we see the ever-growing horizon of the ocean of divine tenderness; and we become ashamed even to mention the pool of our love that lies far away in the vale beneath. Besides, we come to see that all true love to God is only a reflected gleam of His great love towards us. "We love Him because He first loved us."

There is no sweeter atmosphere in which to live than the perpetual consciousness that God loves us. Like the steady heat of the hot-house producing flowers and fruits amid the frosts of December: so, in this icy world, the genial glow of the love of God experienced perennially by the believer will produce those results which are exotics to this World, though they are native to the soil of the New Jerusalem.

When the Apostle bids us keep ourselves in the love of God, he surely does not mean that we need to exert ourselves to prevent the cessation of God's love toward us. The love of God is without variableness, or shadow of turning. Having loved His own which are in the world, He loves them unto the end. We may rest satisfied that nothing can separate us from the love of God, which is in Jesus Christ our Lord. If we are faithless, He remains faithful. If we wander away into backsliding and coldness, He continues immutably the same. If we, like Peter, deny Him, yet He still looks on us with yearning affection, enough to break our hearts. Oh, clasp this blessed thought to your inner consciousness!—that the love of God is more tenacious than a mother's—"she may forget"—and more lasting than hills or mountains, which "may depart."

But the love of God to us is one thing; and our appreciation and enjoyment of that love is quite another. The one is unalterably the same; while the other is fitful and intermittent. Sometimes we are very sensible of the warm beam of God's love shining blessedly into our souls; at other times we have no such joyous consciousness of His love: but we must remember that God's love to us does not in any way depend on our consciousness of it. It is not most, because we happen to feel it most; or least, because we have almost ceased to feel it at all. The one is no gauge of the amount of the other. God's love to us is ever constant, however much our appreciation of it may vary. When the sunlight beams seem to touch only a rim of the moon's surface, we do not argue that the sun is growing cold and dark. When a child wanders far afield from home and mother, we do not suppose that the love has necessarily died out in that mother's heart.

Nevertheless, though our consciousness of God's love does not determine its amount or constancy, yet it is very delightful and helpful to realize it always. Thus we become most sensitive to sin. Thus we acquire purity of heart. Thus we become strong and fearless. Thus, too, we become magnetic, attracting others to Him who has made us what we are.

May we not live in the hourly consciousness of the love of God toward us?

Is not this what Jesus meant when He said, "I have kept My Father's commandments, and *abide* in His love?" Is not this what He meant, when He bade us keep His commandments and abide in His own love? And what else did Jude mean by bidding his fellow-Christians to keep themselves "in the love of God?"

We may not always or exclusively be dwelling on it; but continually looking up from our work, and finding that that benignant face is still smiling on us; and that that over-arching heaven of love is still above and around; not able to speak much of our love to God, but always able to speak of His love to us—like a child who plays about the house without questioning for a moment, because it feels instinctively that all around it is shining the love of the mother.

There are three or four brief hints that may be of service:—

I. Take time to consider God's love to you. God loves the world, because He loves each unit in the great sum of human life. We see the parterres of spring; to Him each flower is distinct. To us the sparrows are so similar that we cannot distinguish one from the rest; but He marks each sparrow's fall. We stand in wonder beneath the arch of the starry sky, and are bewildered by the multitudinousness of the star-dust. He calls each atom by its separate name. And so when we think of God's love to us, we must not think He loves us as part of the race; but with a special individualizing love, which singles us out of the crowd, as a father loves each child with a love in which no other can share.

"Thou art as much His care, as if beside
    Nor man, nor angel lived in heaven and earth."

This belief in God's personal love is very helpful. It prevents us from feeling lost in a crowd. But it is not natural or easy at first. We must be patient, and take time to allow the thought to possess us, in its mighty grasp. We must get alone, and shut the door upon the busy world, and set ourselves to comprehend the meaning of those three small words, *God loves me.* We must learn that it is of the very nature of an Infinite Being to be as much in one place as though He were in no other place; and to love one lonely heart as if there were none other to share His love in all the wide universe. In the morning, before you enter on the calls of daily duty, take time— five minutes—quietly to realize that you are the object of the deep personal love of the Infinite God.

II. Accept all the incidents of the day as coming from His love. I do not see how we can make distinctions between God's ordaining and His permissive providence, any more than we can between His special and general providence. All life, and its many incidents; what comes to us directly from His hand, equally with what is permitted to happen to us through the means of others— must be traced back to Himself as the ultimate final cause. Our Lord was delivered by the determinate counsel and fore-knowledge of God; though this did not lessen the wickedness of the hands by which He was crucified and slain. Here is the mystery of the ages; but let not the mystery rob us of the undoubted truth, that God is behind all events.

And God is love. All events, therefore, must be consistent with His love. And we must recognize this, if we would keep ourselves in its glad and constant enjoyment. When any bright thing befalls you; when any one says anything kind of you; when an unexpected gift falls at your feet; when a new friendship enters your life; when the sun shines brightly on your path—look up, and know that all lovely and helpful things are the children of the love of God. Do not be so occupied with the gift, or the channel through which it comes, as to ignore the Giver Himself.

And when unkind things are said or done; when robber bands steal your goods, as Job's; when friends disappoint you, and Shimeis curse—then look up, and be sure that all is permitted by a love that cares for you none the less tenderly when it withholds its help. "Jesus loved Martha, and her sister, and Lazarus: when He heard, *therefore*, that he was sick, He abode two days still in the same place where He was."

Thus every event that comes to you will link you, by a golden clasp, with the love of God.

III. Be channels of God's love to others. In the spring, the vine-root, bursting with life-power, longs for branches through which it may pour its tides of life forth to refresh thirsty souls; and surely the love of God is ever seeking for kindred hearts, who shall be channels of communication with the world. The world, too, needs love. There is nothing which can slake its thirst, but the love of God. It will ever thirst again till it drinks of that stream.

Why should not you, my reader, be one of the channels through which God's love may pour itself out to refresh him that is weary? If you are willing, you will find yourself beginning to care for men as never before; and there will be a new power of affection opened within you which shall betray its Divine origin.

And what, think you, shall be the effect of this upon yourself, except to teach you the meaning of God's love to *you?* For the water which flows along a channel can refresh the flowerets that grow upon its banks. Those that live in love to others know the love of God to themselves; and to keep other men in our love is to keep ourselves in the love of God. Forsake wrath, jealousy,

191

and envy, in the power of God's grace, and learn the new, glad lesson of love.

IV. Associate with those who love God. No one of us can know the fulness of God's love in the loneliness of our own communings. We need to associate *with all saints* to learn its height and depth, and length and breadth. It is a mistake to isolate ourselves from communion with Christians, or from corporate Church-life; and it is my earnest advice to all young Christians, as to all secret disciples, to find some happy center of Christian fellowship, and join it.

We see the love of God from different angles. It shines on us with different hues. And no one can fully appreciate it, and its full extent, who has not spoken with other Christians about it, and tried to catch some new beauty in their conceptions. Talk much of the love of God to those around you. Hear them, and ask them questions. So shall your heart burn within you, and Jesus will make Himself known in some deeper, sweeter guise. Christian converse is a great help towards the abiding realization of the love of God.

V. Live in obedience to every known command. "If ye keep My commandments, ye shall abide in My love; as I have kept My Father's commandments, and abide in His love." This is the secret—to search the Word to see if you are keeping all His commands; to seek and keep His laws; to put the government upon His shoulders; to do His will, at whatever cost to self-will; to obey, not to win aught from His hand, but just to please Him; to ask forgiveness and restoration if you have erred or gone astray. Here is the essential condition of walking in the light of His love.

Who has not been conscious of a sweet manifestation of love, when some difficult duty has been done for His dear sake alone? As when Jesus was baptized, the heavens were opened, and the voice of God declared Him to be His beloved Son.

Let us "walk in the light, as He is in the light": so shall we be conscious not of light only, but of love.

There is no need for us to live in a cold and arctic zone, if only we fulfil the conditions here set down. We may not always be equally buoyant, or equally exuberant; or equally responsive; but we shall never lose the bright glad consciousness that we are loved by the Love that spared not the only-begotten Son.